165 67155

THE RAILWAY BUILDERS

THE RAILWAY BUILDERS

*Lives and Works of the Victorian
Railway Contractors*

R. S. JOBY

DAVID & CHARLES
Newton Abbot   London   North Pomfret (Vt)

British Library Cataloguing in Publication Data

Joby, R. S.
   The railway builders.
   1. Railway companies – History – 19th century
   2. Contractors – History – 19th century
   I. Title
   331.7'6251   HD9712

   ISBN 0-7153-7959-3

Typeset by Typesetters (Birmingham) Limited,
and printed in Great Britain
by Redwood Burn Limited, Trowbridge, Wilts
for David & Charles (Publishers) Limited
Brunel House   Newton Abbot   Devon

Published in the United States of America
by David & Charles Inc
North Pomfret   Vermont 05053   USA

Contents

*Dedicated to my wife
and family*

Introduction

Hundreds of sweating, cursing men attack the raw earth with pickaxes and shovels. Earth and rock is heaped into gigantic wheelbarrows which, on a signal from below, jerk up a narrow, slippery plank road, balanced precariously by a sun-tanned and heavily muscled man. A horse led by a boy pulls a frayed rope over a pulley to bring a load of earth to the lip of the cutting where it is dumped before the barrow goes down for more. Further down the cutting the living rock is being torn asunder by gunpowder. The fuse-setters and navvies crouch behind any cover they can find before returning to the job of preparing for the next blast. Everywhere noise, dust and smoke fills the air. Rough-looking gangers drive their butty gangs to ever greater feats of earth-moving by threats, promises and, at times, well-aimed kicks for the pay of the gang depends on the efforts of the team as a whole.

Amid the ant-like activity, a well-dressed man moves about in an assured manner. Gaiters protect his expensive trousers from the muck all around, but judging by his broad hands and burly shoulders he has himself wielded a pickaxe in his time. The contractor has arrived for his weekly inspection of the works, greeting gangers and navvies with a selective *bonhomie*, bestowing a word of praise here, chivvying there, part of his ceaseless round of investigation of the works which are being carried out on a multitude of sites up and down the line, and often further afield. The contractor was the person who had set the men and horses to work, paid the wages, and later in the Railway Age may himself have promoted the line directly or through nominees. He was usually in his element walking purposefully around the construction site, estimating, adjusting, greeting and rebuking by turns. Yet back in town he was often trying hard to develop the social graces and political power to which he felt entitled, thanks to his usually new-found wealth.

Another view of the contractor came from the sometimes acid pen of Anthony Trollope in his novel *Doctor Thorne*. A patient of Doctor Thorne is the railway contractor Sir Roger Scatcherd 'who was whilom a drunken stone-mason in Barchester'. In less than a paragraph Trollope sums up an amalgam of the progress of a successful Victorian railway contractor: 'He had become a contractor, first for little things, such as half a mile or so of railway embankment, or three or four canal bridges, and then a contractor for great things, such as government hospitals, locks, docks and quays, and had latterly had in his hands the making of whole lines of railway.' Trollope also noted the general arrangements of the business of contracting at the time: 'He had been occasionally in partnership with one man for one thing, and then with another for another; but had, on the whole, kept his own interests to himself, and now, at the time of our story, he was a very rich man.'

The rise of the contractor to national importance was embodied in Sir Roger:

> There had been a time when the government wanted the performance of some extraordinary piece of work, and Roger Scatcherd had been the man to do it. There had been some extremely necessary bit of railway to be made in half the time that such work would properly demand, some speculation to be incurred requiring great means and courage as well, and Roger Scatcherd had been found to be the man for the time. He was then elevated for the moment to the dizzy pinnacle of a newspaper hero . . . He went up one day to court to kiss her Majesty's hand, and came down to his grand new house at Boxall Hill, Sir Roger Scatcherd, Bart.[1]

Within the fictional character were elements of the two greatest contractors, Peto and Brassey, although neither started as humble stonemasons, nor were they drunkards. They performed some of the extraordinary feats and Peto became a baronet, but many elements of Scatcherd were pure fiction.

The contractor was often viewed by his established social superiors as a gatecrasher, portrayed as vulgar in satirical magazines, yet courted and cultivated by engineers, financiers and others who stood to gain by his acquaintance, through those skills of man and money management which the best of them possessed, together with that manic energy which enabled them to control a huge and fractious work-force operating in many parts of the country or the world. The contractors built up to and beyond the bounds of existing constructional knowledge, and were regarded by some popular journalists as heroes of Victorian capitalism. On the other hand, that inimitable and at times eccentric railway manager, Sir Edward Watkin, could say before his shareholders in 1872 that 'at the opera, if we look at the lady occupants of the best boxes, who are glittering with the best diamonds, and ask who they are, we are told that they are the wife and daughters of Clodd the great railway contractor'. This jaundiced view came from one who fancied that contractors often got the better of the railways in their bargaining, ignoring the host of bankrupt casualties of the system. The fictitious Clodd was doing very nicely and was not afraid to show it, but many of his kind had been consumed in the waves of financial instability that periodically overwhelmed the great Victorian booms of mid-century.

The engineers and the architects tend to receive most of the credit for designing and having built the structures and earthworks that went to make our British railways, but without the special skills of the contractors in assembling the men, the materials and the bank credits to carry the paper plans to completion, the drawings of the engineers and architects would have remained on paper only. The result of the teamwork between engineer and architect on the one hand and the contractor, mason, ganger and navvy on the other, was a heritage of routes, structures and buildings that form a large part of our Victorian endowment. Until recently it was fashionable to deride railway structures. Now a more enlightened attitude is resulting in a greater appreciation of the physical creations of the age of the railway engineer and contractor.

The railway contractor was faced with numerous novel problems, of a size and complexity never before tackled. Thinking big became normal by the 1830s, extending nationwide in the following decade. The iron and glass Crystal Palace of Paxton and Fox paved the way for the construction of the massive train sheds of the 1850s and 1860s. These advanced structures were also highly decorative in many cases, and the contractors used their ability to utilise a wide variety of materials to good effect by, for example, laying bricks in a decorative way. The resultant buildings and structures have generally not only been durable but adaptable as well, today being used for loads unthought of at the time of their construction, unimaginable traffic densities and speeds which represent as big a stride forward from those of early Victorian railways, as their own fastest trains did from stage-coaches. Even the radical alterations necessary for electrification have often been accommodated within Victorian structures. There was also poor quality work, but inspection and time have eliminated much that was bad in Victorian construction, leaving us with a basic network of railways solidly built and of considerable historical interest.

The network of main lines that is still largely with us today was built between 1837 and 1852. Thereafter, although there were numerous additions to the systems of most railways and also several smaller railways that had not started construction in 1852, the period of manic investment and construction was already over by this date, and the richer members of the British public no longer thought of railway shares as a route to a quick fortune. This raised numerous problems when it came to financing new lines, to the extent that Richard Moon, chairman of the mighty London & North Western Railway, said to his shareholders in 1862: 'There is not one of the great companies in this country who can raise sixpence without preference or guaranteed shares. There are no proprietors willing to come forward to make a railway. They are made by contractors, engineers and speculators, who live on the fears of the companies.' He was probably exaggerating for effect, but certainly there was little gain to be had by a main line company in diluting its share capital when having branch lines constructed. Yet failure to do so inevitably meant that the local gentry would have a plausible case for approaching a rival company to build a line into their district with the help of a contractor and his financial associates. The histories of the London, Chatham & Dover Railway and the Midland & Great Northern Railway are full of just such activity.

Railway lines built between 1825–45

Whether the later construction was fully justified or not, it happened. By 1872 the pioneering days of construction sites resembling animated ant colonies and lengthy new main and secondary lines were drawing to a close. The great contractors who had survived the recurrent crises had drawn appropriate conclusions on the subject of self-preservation. Their companies had diversified their interests and broadened their structures in such a way that organisations of the kind that Peto and Brassey had founded ceased to exist, and there was little danger of the economic holocaust of 1866 being repeated, when a large number of contractors, including Peto, failed.

Railway lines built between 1845–54

The best railway contractors were also the master builders of their age. The Cubitts, John Kelk, the Lucases and the McAlpines, Weetman Pearson and Thomas Walker all constructed far more than railways. Even Peto and Brassey were not exclusively railway contractors. It was they who introduced the new constructional materials on a vast scale: wrought iron, cast iron, steel and new types of brick that they knew after experiment would be best for the work. They scoured the country for suitable materials at times of peak output, their orders helping to make Peterborough Flettons and Ibstock bricks known nationally, and the works there to grow prodigiously in size. The railways that they built conveyed the new products to all parts of the country, and the new lines to suburbs and resorts encouraged demand for building products in their turn. It was no coincidence that John Kelk and Charles Lucas built the Metropolitan District Railway while at the same time developing both the private and public building in the districts served by that line. As the new building materials became more widely known, so local materials of inferior quality were phased out. In remote Melton Constable, atop the ridge of central Norfolk, building was in local Norfolk Red Brick until the 1880s, after which the railways brought the ubiquitous and cheaper Fletton brick to construct more watertight houses for the railwaymen there.

The most noted examples of the builder's craft on the railways are the great structures which bestride valleys and inlets, estuaries and ravines. The solid masonry or brick arch has become almost a cliché for the Victorian viaduct or bridge, with many more in cast and wrought iron or timber, and late in the century the concrete arches of the McAlpines on the West Highland line. The timber and cast iron has largely vanished through maintenance problems and increasing loads, but wrought-iron bridges designed by Stephenson and Brunel, and largely constructed by Fairbairn, still carry heavy traffic after more than a century including the Conwy bridge in North Wales, while Arrol's steel cantilevers in Scotland remain landmarks in early steel construction. Their erection was the wonder of the age; their destruction would be pure vandalism.

British railway stations were very mixed in quality and size when built. The best usually occur in groups on lines where someone on the board cared about good architecture or was out to create a favourable impression. There is still an especially fine group on the Ipswich & Bury Railway line in Suffolk, including Needham Market and Stowmarket, constructed by Brassey in 1846, while those between Newport (Essex) and Norwich, built around the same time by Peto, include the magnificent Cambridge station with its *porte cochère*, and the black flint station houses at Brandon and Trowse, still happily with us. The number which have withstood neglect until preservation orders could rescue them is testimony to the original solidity of construction. On a larger scale, the major cities and junctions boast outstanding examples of daring and substantial contracting in a quantity and on a scale that made the 1850s and 1860s in particular, landmark years for station building. Just how well built they were came to light in the 1960s when demolition gangs went to work on redundant examples. Cubitt's Euston Arch proved very intractable, its huge stone blocks bonded with lead. In the absence of explosives, demolition time was very protracted. Even humble bridges have proved difficult. The abutments of the bridge across Aylsham Road, North Walsham, were constructed in 1898 by William Mousley. Attempts to blow up the foundations proved fruitless so that a job scheduled to take one day lengthened to a fortnight as the demolition men attacked the abutments brick by brick with sledge-hammers.

One of the main reasons for the quality of so much of the contractors' work was that when they built, their materials – iron, steel, bronze, brass, bricks, timber and glass – had never been cheaper. They could be obtained and delivered in quantity at low cost and erected quickly by a very highly productive labour force. The result was a lavish use of resources under a strict inspection system that rarely failed to ensure that the work was done properly. Most British lines were expensive to build in comparison with those in geographically similar parts of the world. The massive earthworks, country stations like manor houses and even minor structures built to last a century, had few counterparts elsewhere, but they put up the cost of building to over £20,000 per mile for main lines in the mid-nineteenth century and over £10,000 per mile even for single-track branch lines, except under the most favourable conditions.

The least well-constructed lines were those of purely local importance with local directors, light railways, industrial lines and those on which the contractor was under orders to build as cheaply as the Board of Trade would allow on inspection. Light railways in particular had ugly corrugated-iron buildings, hurtful to the eye and fortunately not enduring. The cheaply constructed stations on the East Norfolk Railway were rushed up by Charles Lucas in 1874 on a contract far from his London base and were very poor in comparison with John Waddell's more careful work on the extension of that line. The level-crossing keepers' cottages on the Eastern & Midlands Railway, built to a standard design by Wilkinson & Jarvis, were often of such poor bricks that they had to be replaced in the early years of this century. Other larger railways had reason to rue their penny pinching and slack supervision. The Tay Bridge disaster was but the tip of an iceberg of malpractice which cost such lines dearly in later replacements or running costs. Where the contractor set his own terms and supervised his own work with a nominated board, as did Peto with the East Suffolk Railway and Brassey with the Portsmouth Direct line, then the result was a helter-skelter succession of inadequate earthworks pitching and tossing across country on a line poorly adapted to modern high speed running.

Earthworks have, apart from those altered by line widening, largely stood for more than a century. Those in the soft clays and quicksands of the south east of England have probably needed more attention than elsewhere, largely for geological reasons. For example the London & Southampton Railway's desire to avoid tunnels, steep gradients and any but the most open curves, resulted in earthworks which have collapsed from time to time after exceptionally heavy rain. The South Eastern Railway's coastal line from Folkestone to Dover has given much trouble because of the tendency of the Gault Clay to give way under heavy loading when wet, while the Tonbridge to Hastings line is an engineer's nightmare with its rapidly changing geology and frequent earthworks and tunnels in unstable rock. The deep chalk cuttings which were such a feature of the Hull & Barnsley Railway near Hull, and of the LB&SCR, have very steep unfaced walls, often with nearly vertical faces, resulting in occasional rock falls. Otherwise the main lines of Britain were well constructed and many apparent faults in earthworks appear to have been due to lack of understanding of the geology rather than any deliberate scamping of the work through insufficient excavation or underpinning. The contrast between the way in which most railway lines have stood up to ever-increasing traffic with fortitude, while the M1 motorway has had to be largely rebuilt after a mere two decades serves to illustrate the point.

The evolution of the great railway contractor in the nineteenth

century laid the foundations for the modern international firms
of which Weetman Pearson's was an early modern example. It
was a very effective model, solidly based in several different
kinds of construction and with the financial resources to
withstand even major setbacks. The one-man show which had
dominated the middle of the century gave way to a firm which
still depended on a dynamic principal and a body of reliable
agents for its momentum, but in which no one was absolutely
indispensable, as had been Brassey and Peto in their
organisations. Each agent was in charge of his contract, but he
was usually salaried and replaceable. The devotion to duty of the
management was as strong as it had ever been. Hours were what
the job required, which at peak periods was around the clock and
often around the calendar as well, because deadlines seem to be
an inseparable part of contracting. Time limits set by
parliaments, climates, shareholders or delivery dates have tested
contractors' resources since they began. Only the toughest
survived and late delivery still plagues the industry. Cajoling,
bullying, charming and at times deceiving are part of the stock in
trade of the contractor and his agents. They have had, over the
years, to cope with a more selective and increasingly multinational work-force. The gradual movement from the rough
conditions of the 1840s to the hutted camps, mobile schools,
missions and dispensaries which had been achieved by the turn
of the century, have been subsequently further developed to the
point where the contractor's camp at Sullom Voe in the
Shetlands, built for North Sea oil development, offers a standard
of living far superior to that of the native Shetlanders, not to
mention pay on a lavish scale. Twentieth-century man has more
choice than the dispossessed peasants who flocked to the works
in the nineteenth century.

Danger has always been a major consideration on construction
sites. The parsimony of the early contractors and railway
companies, only too anxious to avoid responsibility for the
numerous accidents in cuttings and tunnels, on bridges and
embankments, was replaced over the years by tighter controls
and safer conditions as contractors were forced to assume more
responsibility and provide safety equipment. But it is still an

industry that ranks with coal mining and deep-sea fishing as one of major risk.

British railway contractors were pioneers in so many directions, both at home and overseas, that they left an imprint of vast dimensions all over the world. The expansion of their work in the middle of the nineteenth century appears reckless in retrospect. Financial markets and some governments were discredited in the wake of that whirlwind of activity and the scandals it left behind, yet from it flowed the agricultural and mineral riches which kept British industry expanding right up to the 1920s. British-built railways ordered British equipment, as did the British-owned farms and mines that they served. The British-built cities had British-built sewers, gasworks and tramways, the hallmarks of a civilisation in which steam locomotive and steamship were the prime movers. Although German, American, French and Australian contractors took many of the major contracts as the nineteenth century progressed, so vast had been the expansion triggered off by the British contractors' initiative that there was still work aplenty, especially for those implementing new inventions. The creative originality of Pearson's Tehuantepec Railway across southern Mexico in 1903 foreshadowed the use of railways as container bridges between oceans in our own time. His use of the Greathead Shield in tunnelling led to one of the few British contracts in the United States when his men burrowed under the Hudson River. Rapid-transit systems below cities were largely British in inspiration and often construction. Others have learned well the lessons of how to organise huge construction sites and some have improved on the British model with the use of a highly disciplined military-type labour force. But it was in Britain during the period of railway construction that the ideas on how to do this were put together and made to work. That breakthrough was then spread far and wide with the gospel of economic progress, through improved communications and better distribution of goods.

The railway contractors took an industry of spades and wheelbarrows in the 1830s and made it, often by trial and error, into an industry of huge dimensions and massive mechanisation by the end of the century. They covered their own country and many overseas as well, with a web of iron and steel that laid the foundations of the advanced commerce of the twentieth century, thereby enriching themselves and their countrymen. By the late nineteenth century the methods of organising construction firms had been laid.

The ancestors of the modern giants, McAlpine, Wimpey, Monk and Mowlem were all at work as railway sub-contractors, building branch lines in remote parts, making short cuts to main lines, new suburban lines, doubling existing tracks, or finishing off cross-country links in that last great burst of railway construction that changed the route maps of the Great Western and Great Central railways.

Railway navvies have been celebrated in print these many years. Now it is the turn of those who directed their labours with flair, daring and sometimes with more than a touch of chicanery.

1

Ancestors of the Railway Contractors

The pedigree of the railway contractor can be traced back to the contractors of the eighteenth century who, albeit on a smaller scale, first organised the building of canals and tramroads using specialist diggers—the navigators or navvies as they became known to the populace.

Until the eighteenth century even the grandest structures were built by methods that differed widely from later ways. Time was far less important when constructing cathedrals designed to last for eternity. In former times the architects or master builders hired the workmen themselves. The labourers were usually local, whereas the craftsmen were usually itinerant, wandering from job to job as opportunity arose. It was only with the slave gangs of ancient Mediterranean and China, as well as the mass-construction of fortresses in Wales under Edward I, that we get a hint of what started to become normal in the canal era, the serial building of massive works with trained migrant labour.

The construction of vast undertakings required the employment of hundreds and later thousands of men along many miles of route, with gangs working at different points simultaneously to a common end. The Great Wall of China and the Roman road system had used forced labour for their construction. This was not available in the European Age of Enlightenment, so an army of strong labourers under a unified command had to be tempted to abandon their normal pursuits to engage in navvying.

The essential requirements of early transport contractors were that they should be able to recruit, supply, pay and control a large army of strong, hard-working diggers. The contractor himself had to be able to follow the instructions of architect and engineer, however inadequate his own education. Most canals and tramroads were constructed with money raised from subscribers who wanted to see a return as soon as possible, so time was the other major factor in the equation. Parliamentary Acts sanctioning construction also contained time clauses, to prevent any group obtaining an Act to build a canal or railway merely to thwart another group from constructing. Thus the scene was set for rapid building of hundreds of miles of canals and tramroads in many parts of the country. Large amounts of money were at stake, so the employment of incompetents who gave low quotations but whose work would have to be done again was not to be recommended.

At first, canal engineers had only relatively small works in hand and recruited local labour on each section of the canal, but the size of the undertakings increased beyond the capacity of an engineer both to plan and supervise individuals. What was needed was a tough, intelligent man to recruit and direct groups of labourers, taking care of details with which the engineer did not wish to concern himself. Payment was on a piece-work basis to the contractor, so much for each cubic yard of soil or rock dug or tipped. The contractor then organised his own workmen, taking a profit if he had estimated accurately. In the 1760s, this was the limit of contracting, but as the size of projects grew and the range of services of contractors likewise expanded, they also extended their work-force to include craftsmen, and the construction of the more complex parts of canals such as tunnels and locks became included in their repertoire. The early history of contracting was very much of a look-and-learn kind but it was the nursery for the even greater contracting that was to come from the late eighteenth century onwards.

In the late 1760s contractors were taking on work valued at a few hundred pounds for the whole of their contract, which itself was likely to be but a small part of the total canal. By the 1780s they were dealing with contracts valued in tens of thousands of pounds and the largest of them controlled hundreds of navvies. Yet many of the contractors themselves, even in the later period, were illiterate and itinerant; they did, however, have the knowledge and the skill to create the wonders of the age. Once they had proved themselves, they were much in demand by other promoters elsewhere, often at a great distance. They started to take on two or more jobs simultaneously, leaving those that they were not personally attending to at a given moment to a trusted deputy, often a son, nephew or brother. This was truly the start of the giant multi-site contractor.

One of the earliest canal contractors was John Pinkerton, who started his contracting career together with his brother on the Driffield Navigation in east Yorkshire as early as 1768. For the next thirty-one years, at first with his brother and later by himself, he contracted to build sections of canals throughout Yorkshire, the West Midlands, the Basingstoke Canal in Hampshire and the Gloucester & Berkeley Canal alongside the Severn, while with John Murray, he took contracts on the Lancaster Canal. In only the smallest of these did he have the whole contract for the canal, which given his workmanship was just as well. Although he might have sounded like a forerunner of Morton Peto or Joseph Firbank in the following century, neither his role nor his resources matched theirs.

The financing of canals was still at a simple level. Calls were made on the resources of shareholders from whose money the company doled out advances to the contractors, who then paid for materials and labour. Either the company loaned the necessary spades, wheelbarrows, ladders, wood for shoring and other items, or these were supplied by an established contractor. Pinkerton started small and borrowed equipment, enlisting his labour locally. His profit depended on how much he could get for the work done and how little he could pay for the use of equipment and manpower. As there is much evidence to suggest that he scamped his work in many places, using either poor or insufficient materials, his continued progress would appear to have been at the expense of his employers. Locks had to be rebuilt after use, the banks of the Basingstoke Canal collapsed, while his work on the Sussex Ouse failed owing to the use of poor materials, and he created great distress in Lancashire by his carelessness in getting men and materials to and from the Lancaster Canal across fields. Yet the frequency with which he was re-employed indicates the even greater inadequacy of other contemporary contractors. He survived lawsuits and the animosity of engineers, having in total some thirty-one years of contracting, a length of career that many later contractors would have envied.

Two father and son teams working mostly in South Wales, the Sheasbys and the Dadfords, provided a much less fraught picture of eighteenth-century contracting. They were also engineers – an early demonstration of the thin line that divided the really competent contractor from the engineer able also to handle men and money. The elder Thomas Dadford was an engineer who had turned contractor and partnered Thomas Sheasby in contracting for the Cromford Canal in 1789 in Derbyshire. The greater opportunities in South Wales the following year caused both families to migrate westwards and act as both contractors and engineers simultaneously in the construction of the Glamorganshire Canal from Cardiff to Merthyr Tydfil, followed by the other four major canals in South Wales linking the valleys to Swansea, Neath and Newport as well as Cardiff by 1799. The size of the contracts, totalling nearly £½m, the vast number of locks, several short tunnels and much masonry, earthmoving and bridge construction, all completed in record time, showed just how far the art of contracting had progressed. But what was even more remarkable was that a nearly equal mileage of tramroads had been completed simultaneously, much of the mileage in Gwent by the younger Dadfords, others by Hodgkinson, Overton and Wells. The transformation of the South Wales valleys from pastoral quiet to frantic industrial activity within a decade was largely due to the speed and competence of the engineer contractors, without whose transport system such progress could not have been made.

The work of the Dadfords and Sheasbys in South Wales also highlighted several practices that they used and were later to become commonplace. Collectively they subscribed only a tenth of the capital of the Aberdare Canal in order to speed promotion of the venture. They employed navvies from distant parts of Wales in the construction of the Monmouthshire Canal at a time when expansion of local industry and the multiplicity of contracts in South Wales necessitated the sucking in of resources from outside the district. They also worked in later years with

George Overton on tramway construction, thus directly linking them with the engineer of the Stockton & Darlington Railway and all that followed from the momentous opening of what was either a late example of a tramway road or the first modern railway, according to one's point of view.

The construction of the Grand Junction Canal from London to Leicester in the 1790s was another pointer to the future. The engineer, William Jessop, let the contract for the great Braunston Tunnel to a partnership of contractors, Jones & Biggs, while on the whole route there were 3,000 navvies at work simultaneously in 1793. He even attempted, unsuccessfully, to save manpower by substituting a manually powered boring machine. The engineer still had to supervise contractors rigorously, but the size of the undertakings, the huge labour forces and the need to specialise pointed the way towards the later system.

Another prominent canal contractor and engineer who made great contributions to the construction and improvement of tramroads was Benjamin Outram. He partnered William Jessop in running the Butterley Ironworks whose rails were used for the Peak Forest Tramroad in 1794. He paid particular attention to easy, continuous gradients suitable for horse traction, and where this was impossible, advocated the steep inclined plane. Good drainage and foundations for the track were also stressed by this pioneer. His other great contribution was his championing of a standard gauge for tramroads, which he foresaw as eventually meeting to become part of a wider system. The gauge chosen was 4ft 2in, remarkably close to the eventual standard gauge.

The other great training grounds for contractors were in the construction of roads and public works in the first decades of the nineteenth century. Both in their architecture and engineering, roads surveyed by that giant of highway construction, Thomas Telford, were on a totally different scale from anything that had been made before.

Thomas Telford also operated his contracts in a new way. He called for competitive tenders. In order to prevent engineer and contractor from arranging matters to their own benefit, he laid down strictly defined responsiblities for each. In this way he was ahead of his time. The new railways did not receive the benefits of his methods until the late 1830s when they were practised on the Grand Junction Railway, where a few large contracts were let to major contractors, the post of engineer being separated as much as possible.

The docks of London and Liverpool, the gas and water undertakings in the larger cities, and massive public buildings all needed agglomerations of labourers and craftsmen on a huge scale, able to respond to the engineer's demands. Armies of navvies were beyond the resources of single regions, except the larger cities, so the process of enticing them into other districts with high wages had to start. James Brindley could find six hundred men in the immediate neighbourhood when constructing the Bridgewater Canal in the 1760s, but 3,000 men in the agricultural Midlands were much harder to find. The migrant navvy was able to work faster than an average labourer and knew what to do without further training, making him more economical to use than the ill-fed surplus labour of the locality, whose chief virtue was that, if employed, they would not be a charge on the local rates. Certainly by the beginning of the nineteenth century there must have been some 70,000 navvies at work on canal, road and tramroad construction, probably topping the 100,000 mark if other public works are considered. A considerable proportion of this force would move on to other similar work when a contract finished, not being established in any town or village, let alone any other trade. Here was the nucleus of that army of constructors which multiplied further with the coming of the railways.

The labour for the contractors came from all parts of the British Isles, but a significant proportion from the 1790s onwards came from those sources traditional thereafter—Ireland and the Scottish Highlands. Amongst the latter was John Aird, father of the great contractor whose work we will later examine. Many others rose from the ranks of the labour force to become contractors both great (albeit few in number) and small. At an early stage the problems of feeding and accommodating navvies on the job came to the fore, with few solutions being offered. The crude huts that the Scottish and Irish peasants were used to at home sufficed for them in England; food and drink were obtained where and when available, while entertainment was by their own fellows or roving singers. A rough and ready life, easy come easy go, was already the hallmark of the navvy in the early years of the new century.

Just as the railway or canal navvy who shifted the soil and rock was so very different from the typical British labourer of the construction period of our national transport system, so the railway contractor was a larger than life version of the sub-contractor who had started the process in the middle of the eighteenth century. A contractor was originally a man who gathered labourers and often supplied them with tools, offering to undertake earth-moving for a set sum related to the size of the job. At a more sophisticated level, a mason and his team would offer to construct a bridge, miners to burrow a tunnel. These small teams were supervised by the engineer in charge of canal, tramroad or turnpike and were paid as the work progressed. This was a far cry from the great railway contractors of the middle of the nineteenth century, several of whom were millionaires, operating nationally and internationally on a grand scale. Yet it was from small beginnings that contractors and their work-forces learned the increasingly complex task of tendering for and completing railway lines whose scale has only been matched in this century by motorway construction. From simple beginnings, illiterate gangs under illiterate masters were modified until British contractors and their navvies were sought to build railways in all continents. They also developed financial expertise, eventually conceiving as well as constructing railways.

2
Pioneering Days

The industrial expansion of south Lancashire in the early nineteenth century resulted in the cities of Manchester and Liverpool attracting populations which made them respectively the second and third largest urban areas in the country. They replaced Bristol and Norwich in this respect, hitherto the greatest provincial cities. The traffic that they generated in both goods and passengers soon proved inadequate for the existing roads and waterways. Thus it was that the merchants of the two boom cities sought to build a railway between them in order to remove a bottleneck to growth that was becoming embarrassing.

Although railways had made considerable progress in the first quarter of the nineteenth century, even the Stockton & Darlington Railway of 1825 was still built and run largely in the manner of the older tramroads. The railway between the two major northern industrial cities was planned on a much larger scale, was run by practical businessmen determined to control their expensive enterprise very tightly.

The Act to build the Liverpool & Manchester Railway (L&MR) was only granted after a titanic struggle in Parliament against the waterway interests and landowners. The direct route surveyed by Charles Vignoles was across peat bog and through sandstone ridges. The directors wished to control construction of the line rather than entrust it to others who might not perform as required. Although the greatest of the canals, the Grand Junction Canal, was both longer and had consumed more capital, the L&MR was the largest scheme yet for railway construction.

The plan for the L&MR provided for a really well-graded trackbed by cutting direct across treacherous mosses instead of skirting them. There were to be well-built terminal stations in the centre of the two cities, unlike the ancestral tramroads which served mines and ports, while earthworks, bridges and other civil engineering features were on a liberal scale, resulting in a cost of £17,000 per mile, a sum hitherto unheard of in tramroad and primitive railway construction, where £2,000 per mile had been normal. This sum paid for the removal and emplacement of 5,000,000 cubic yards of soil, much masonry, ironwork and brickwork besides. Most of the work was done by muscle and hand tools. This was Britain's, indeed the world's, first inter-city railway. For such lines there was an end to contour-hugging and minimal earthworks; the Liverpool & Manchester Railway was on a grand scale and so was its impact on the nation.

Railways of the tramroad type continued to be built for many years after the L&MR had pioneered the methods of building main-line railways, and several of the older type survived into the present century, but their purpose was largely confined to mineral traffic and their impact local, especially where they were of a different gauge or not compatible with the Stephenson model of railway building which quickly triumphed after 1830.

George Stephenson was appointed Chief Operative Engineer of the L&MR after much argument, a grandiloquent title later simplified to Principal Engineer. He appointed his own resident engineers to oversee construction on the spot, including his former apprentice Joseph Locke and his surveyor on two previous lines, John Dixon. They in turn had oversight of superintendents who carried out specific projects on the line such as bridges and tunnels. Not only did Stephenson select his own technical hierarchy, but also some of his more specialised workers and navvies who included Geordies, Lancastrians and Irishmen. By making sure that he knew his team, he was able to supervise their efforts with greater confidence, and could delegate without fear when business took him to other sites both in Lancashire and elsewhere. Being first had its disadvantages in that there was no model based on railway experience to copy, but it did give him the pick of available talent and provided an invaluable training ground for some of those directing later projects.

George Stephenson appears to have learned little from his predecessors on major canal- or road-building contracts. Those who contracted for him were usually rough-cut foremen and gangers who took on small lengths of the line, always under a mile, working under the direction of George Stephenson and his son Robert, who became his father's chief assistant on many new projects. George himself acted as both engineer and chief contractor, an unhealthy situation. Although he was personally honest, George Stephenson did not provide a model for future construction work that could be followed by others in a fast expanding industry where rogues abounded.

Below the level of personally selected workers, local contractors and their men were brought in, usually through newspaper advertisements, to bid for specific sub-contracts. The terms were usually in pence per cubic yard of material removed or emplaced, the latter being worth about twice the former. The work was performed with simple tools and gunpowder, even when cutting through rock. The loosened material was loaded into small trucks on a portable tramway for disposal.

The number employed on any one site was up to 280. Work proceeded simultaneously at several points along the route and at both ends of Olive Mount cutting. All sites were co-ordinated by Stephenson for much of the time, as he spent up to nine months a year on this, his most important job to date. The resident engineers acted in his absence, but could not have had such a full overview. They also acted as paymasters to their direct employees and the sub-contracting gangs. They collected wages fortnightly from the company office in Liverpool, simultaneously making progress reports which informed the directors, who could then query any failure to meet targets. The controls exercised must have been effective as the railway was completed within its financial target, despite the problems of Chat Moss and Olive Mount cutting, while the date of opening was only a few months behind the optimistic hopes of 1826.

Accidents were fewer than expected, delays due to adverse weather rather longer than hoped for, but completion was to the general satisfaction of most concerned, a signal achievement when one considers the magnitude of the task and the number of novel problems overcome. The sub-contractors were paid over £250,000, probably representing over one million man days, which gives the measure of the co-ordination needed to prevent overlap and muddle. Bonuses were awarded to sub-contractors who kept work going under difficult conditions, and fines exacted for late completions.

George Stephenson and his assistants had engineered their first two lines from survey to completion in the case of the Stockton & Darlington, and from laying out of the line to completion in the case of the Liverpool & Manchester Railway, as well as providing locomotives and carrying out a number of other assignments simultaneously. It was a measure of the shortage of men able and willing to control such vast and novel enterprises that he had so much to do, as did Brindley at a similar stage in the canal-building era. As larger railways were proposed, some further development of the chain of command became inevitable. How that developed we shall see later, but a person whose railway contracting started at this time was Thomas Brassey, who supplied building stone for Sankey Viaduct from quarries that he managed locally. His speedy and honest performance of this task marked him as someone to be used on a future occasion.

After opening, the L&MR proved a financial and operating success, which was quickly imitated by the promotion of large numbers of schemes usually linking pairs of towns in several parts of the country. This period has since become known as the first Railway Mania. Chief among the lines projected and later built in the 1830s were the London & Birmingham Railway, the Grand Junction Railway, linking the L&MR with Birmingham, the North Midland Railway from Leeds to Derby, the Great Western Railway from London to Bristol, the London & Southampton Railway, the Newcastle & Carlisle Railway and the Edinburgh & Glasgow Railway to mention only the most important. Those which were built before the second Railway Mania multiplied the national railway mileage from the original disconnected series of short lines. The Stephensons were prominent in the building of the first three railways, using the methods that had been so successful on the L&MR. On the larger scale, the use of a multitude of sub-contractors was less than successful, whereas on the same Grand Junction Railway, George Stephenson's pupil Joseph Locke developed the new idea of having a few or even only a single contractor, responsible to the engineer for building a complete section or even a whole railway. He took the idea a stage further on the London & Southampton Railway where he had to complete a partly built railway, one that had started in the way approved by George Stephenson with contracts 'given in small lots to small men, at a low price'.[1] The result was that there, as on the London & Birmingham Railway, the easier parts of the work were completed, leaving a trail of failure and bankruptcy when the work got difficult in country needing major earthworks or tunnelling.

Until the mid-1830s the mileage of railways authorised in any one year rarely exceeded 200. As the projects of the first Railway Mania matured into royal assents to build and raise capital, the annual mileage leapt to nearly 1,000 miles. Since much of the mileage already authorised had not yet been built there were some 1,500 miles of line to be built or in course of construction by 1836. Here was demand for contractors and their men on a scale never met before and in places where even tramroads had never been seen before. Experienced engineers were few, their resources already overstretched. Contractors of substance with railway experience were even fewer. Those that existed were men who had sub-contracted for a few miles of line or a major viaduct or earthwork. There existed a nucleus of contractors such as Hugh McIntosh, the Nowell family and William Hoof who had experience in building tramroads, public works, docks, roads, bridges or the later canals, but the potential volume of work far outstripped the numbers available, resulting in in-experienced men taking on far larger contracts than in the past. The results varied from a new standard of excellence to disastrous. Robert Stephenson engaged twenty-nine contractors to build the London & Birmingham Railway with contract lengths of only 6 miles each, reserving large individual structures such as viaducts, tunnels and major stations to the most reliable firms, but there were several costly failures, the Kilsby Tunnel being the worst of them.

The key man in the Stephenson type of contracting was the engineer, who by the time he came to allocate contracts, had already surveyed the line and alternatives in detail, attended parliament to fight for the Act to build the railway after submitting an estimate of the cost of the line, had plans drawn up for all structures and taken trial borings for tunnels and major earthworks. A contemporary description continues:

> This mass of information having been prepared, the chief engineer now advertises his work in its various lengths for execution by contract, and on receiving tenders for the same, he selects, not always the lowest, but that which, for various reasons, is the most approved, taking security generally to the amount of 10% of the contract.
>
> Previous, however, to the reception of the tenders the chief engineer appoints his staff of assistants. To each 40 or 50 miles there is usually appointed an experienced engineer, having under him 'sub-assistants', who superintend from 10 to 15 miles each – these sub-assistants being again assisted by 'inspectors' of masonry, of mining, of earthwork, and of permanent way, to each of whom a particular district is assigned.
>
> The chief engineer now finds himself engaged in a new struggle with man in addition to nature. In many cases the contractors let out a portion of the work they have engaged to perform to sub-contractors, who again 'set' the earth-work to a body of 'navvies' who again among themselves sub-divide it among the three branches of which their State is composed, namely 'excavators', 'trenchers', and 'runners', each party of whom employ their own 'ganger'.
>
> The duty of effectively overlooking all these details, of preventing collusion as well as collision, of enforcing the due execution of the contract, and yet, where necessary, occasionally to alleviate the strict letter of its law, constitute perhaps the most harassing of the various difficulties which the chief engineer has to overcome; for it must be evident that if, by means of bribery, or from inattention, or from sheer roguery, any important portion of the work be 'scamped' or insufficiently performed, results may ere long occur of the most serious description.[2]

Under such a system, the chief engineer was constantly patrolling the line being built. As the work expanded by the mid-1830s, the assistants and sub-assistants were less and less trained to carry out their tasks, while the contractors being employed were sometimes just not up to the job when emergencies arose. There were hundreds of small firms at work all over the country, very few of them with the financial reserves or engineering knowledge to carry on when faced with such problems as were encountered in the construction of the Watford and Kilsby tunnels on the London & Birmingham Railway. In

the latter case, a body of quicksand had been missed in the trial
borings, resulting in a delay of eight months of the opening of
the line, the death of the contractor Joseph Nowell who on
hearing the news had 'instantly taken to his bed', the death of
twenty-six men and a tripling of the cost from the original
estimate of £99,000. Nowell was apparently already a sick man in
the early stages of the contract. The result was that Robert
Stephenson and his assistants had to take over construction and
finish the job as they had no confidence in Nowell's sons. Most
contractors of the period just did not have the knowledge to
undertake several kinds of building simultaneously, nor did they
have the capital and the material resources to tackle works in
excess of about £100,000 at the values of the 1830s.

The problems faced at Kilsby by Nowell and Robert
Stephenson were not only of a geological nature. Unlike most
other sites on the L&BR where work proceeded for a few months
and then the navvies struck camp and went to new works, the
length of the construction period at Kilsby meant that 1,250
labourers were resident for lengthy periods and also required the
services of 'sutlers and victuallers' as well as other camp
followers. The conditions of this semi-permanent settlement
were such that 'there lodged in each room sixteen navvies, and
there were four beds in each apartment, two navvies were
actually in each; the two squads of eight men as alternatively
changing places with each other in their beds as in their work'.[3]
In addition to overcrowding the existing village, a large village
was constructed above the tunnel. However, at least the workers
were well fed, it being asserted that 'more beef was eaten at
Kilsby during the construction of the tunnel than had previously
been consumed there since the Deluge'.[4]

The engineer who took command of a contract had to be
doubly watchful of the sub-contractors, who were all too well
aware of how overstretched the great man was. Robert
Stephenson in those days almost lived on the line (during the
building of the L&BR). He thought he detected 'scamping' on
the part of one of his contractors. He sent orders to the man to
meet him on the works, and coming up rapidly as he caught sight
of him burst out, 'so and so, you're a most infernal scoundrel'.

'Well Sir', replied the delinquent, 'I know I am.' Robert
Stephenson dismissed him with a friendly warning.[5]

The resident engineer of the L&BR was Robert B. Dockray,
whose letter books during the construction period are full of tart
missives to contractors, other engineers and suppliers, none of
whom seemed fully up to the mark in his view. One aimed at
Samuel Morton Peto performing his first railway contract gives
an idea of the problems:

> 10 Vauxhall Grove
> Birmingham
> 18 August 1837

My dear Sir,
> I have to request that you will immediately remove the
rejected Coping Stones laying in the Merchandise Department, and
also that you will take some steps to produce others of a proper
quality – I have written Rutherford that I cannot accept a single
stone – no time ought to be lost in finishing the wall before the frost
or wet weather comes on.

> I am my dear Sir,
> Yours very truly,
> Robert B. Dockray.

Another factor that became very apparent during the construction of the early main-line railways was that the estimates
made by the engineers were often very much short of the final
cost of the line. The cost of land on the route from London to
Birmingham exceeded £500,000, parliamentary expenses
gobbled up another £73,000, but these paled into insignificance
against the trebling in cost of Kilsby Tunnel, the doubling of the
cost at Primrose Hill Tunnel, or the even worse escalation of
costs experienced by the London & Southampton Railway. The
engineer to that unfortunate line was Francis Giles, who had
successfully completed the Newcastle & Carlisle Railway in an
area long used to tramroad and primitive railway construction.

In the Newcastle area he had advertised in the *Newcastle
Chronicle* for 'Earthworkers who are wishing to enter into
contracts for executing Excavations and Embankments', who
had to send their tenders to the company solicitors and would
then be shown the work. The contractor in that area, long used
to making and repairing tramroads and colliery workings, would

then 'by some mental progress entirely unintelligible to the educated engineer, name a sum for which he would execute the works comprised in the distance a sum moreover, that would come very close to the estimate of the men of science'.[6]

Such methods worked well in the north of England where excavators were in plentiful supply, but in railway and industrial terms, the south of England was virgin territory; its canals and turnpikes long completed, it lacked a nucleus of competent contractors. The capital of the London & Southampton Railway was set at £1,000,000, a little more than Giles had estimated to be 'fair and feasible'. However, as with the L&BR, problems arose so that 'when any engineering novelty arose, the poor contractor was powerless. The smallest difficulty stayed him; the slightest danger paralysed him. He could not complete his contracts; he lacked the resources to pay the penalty; the works were often stopped; the directors as often in despair.' Brunel too had his problems on the Great Western Railway with contractors going bankrupt in awkward places and at awkward times. Of the railways built in the 1830s, the one that was built at the least cost and with the least delay was the Grand Junction Railway where Joseph Locke took control of the construction of the whole line after George Stephenson bowed out. As a former pupil of Stephenson, he went on to improve on the master's methods, especially in the detailed costing of the line and the letting of contracts. His greatest contribution was in bringing forward the contractor as a much more important figure in both construction and finance of the larger railways then being built.

Although the Grand Junction Railway was the largest single line to have been commenced in the mid-1830s, Locke's choice of contractors was so good that only one seems to have been in default. One Thomas Townsend had taken on four contracts, but Locke had to finish the work for him in 1837. Two of the other contractors to the GJR later became much better known: Samuel Morton Peto of the firm of Grissell & Peto undertook the building of Curzon Street station in Birmingham as their first railway work, together with a similar contract in the same street for the L&BR; further north, Joseph Locke had persuaded Thomas Brassey to alter his submitted tender for the Penkridge contract down to his own estimate, thus starting a career in railway construction for Brassey that never faltered and which bound engineer and contractor in a business framework that spanned the world within two decades. Both were young, extremely energetic and willing to take on responsibility as no one had before in the building of railways.

When Joseph Locke took over the shambles left by Giles on the London & Southampton Railway, he was fortunate in having the backing of William Chaplin, who had previously provided horses for half the mail coaches leaving London. The demonstrable success of railways outside London convinced him that he should support the new medium of transport, so he became a director of the struggling railway and also went into the carrying business from railway terminals. Locke assessed the situation, chose 'able and responsible contractors', including Thomas Brassey, who was given no less than 19 miles of the main line from Basingstoke to Winchester. He later went on to build the Gosport branch and the main line from Basingstoke to Yeovil.

Well-financed and reliable contractors hardly existed in 1830, apart perhaps from McKenzie, the canal contractor who later became Brassey's partner, Thomas Cubitt, a member of the great Norfolk engineering and contracting clan who built the Euston end of the L&BR, as well as much London housing, and Grissell & Peto who had built the Houses of Parliament and became interested in railway construction during the first Railway Mania. By the end of that tumultuous period, Brassey was well enough established to follow Locke to France in order to build the first main-line railway there from Paris to Rouen, while Peto was able to secure the contract to build the entire Yarmouth & Norwich Railway of 22 miles length. It was a time when Darwin's hypothesis of the selection of the fittest might be said to apply to railway contracting.

The contractor who could move from small to large contracts had been discovered, enabling the engineer to deal with far fewer principals, to whom could be delegated much of the detailed recruitment and supervision of labour and the acquisition of materials, thus freeing the engineer for his more professional

duties. Meanwhile the two great trans-Pennine lines from
Manchester to Leeds and to Sheffield were constructed by small
contractors taking small contracts with resultant delays, in
marked contrast to the speed of completion of the London &
Southampton Railway.

The great increase in railway construction had required a
similar increase in the work-force, especially in parts of the
country where an experienced construction force was lacking.
The tempo of railway building increased fivefold in the later
1830s, drawing in thousands of navvies old and new, constantly
replenishing the contractors' labour manifest. The labourer was
recruited to the navvy gang consisting of a dozen or so men
under a ganger, who was himself responsible to a sub-contractor,
who in turn was responsible to the contractor. Local labour,
either unemployed or in search of better pay, farm labourers
from elsewhere with some experience of contracting work and
migrants from the Celtic fringes, generally composed the labour
force. They usually worked in groups from similar areas and
moved on in small groups when a contract was completed. Their
strength and legendary appetites for meat, bread, beer and spirits
marked them out from the average British labourer of the period,
so that new recruits would soon have to prove their work
capacity and stamina if they were to remain successful members
of a gang. The shovel work required the shifting of some 6 cubic
yards of material in a shift, material that could vary from dry
sand to sodden clay. This was then taken up steeply inclined
planes from a cutting bottom in wheelbarrows containing up to
4cwt, another navvy acting to balance the barrow load while a
horse at the top of the plank pulled the barrow upwards. Should
the rope snap or the barrow man lose his balance on the slippery
wood, then anything from bruising to death could happen. The
hours were long, especially in summer, Sundays were often
worked but pay at over £2 a week for an experienced labourer
was four or five times as much as he could get on a farm in the
non-industrial parts of the British Isles. Furthermore, with the
population rising and the number of farm labourers required
falling, there was always a surplus willing to try navvying.

The problem with the navvies lay in the fact that large bodies of men were working in deeply rural areas, far from shops and entertainment, for the most part unprovided with accommodation yet earning large sums by the standards of the time. The typical small contractor was only concerned that they did their work. He was happy to supply the men with food, goods and drink through a shop run by a partner who, having a monopoly, charged high prices for inferior produce. It was necessary that the contractor did not himself run the shop, so as not to contravene the Truck Acts, but by issuing credit tickets only exchangeable at the named shop, the contractor could ensure that his men paid high prices and added to his profits. Robert Stephenson would not allow alcohol to be sold in such shops, but did not stamp out the practice. Only Peto seems to have refused to have any such 'tommy shops' on his contracts.

The navvies were paid at different intervals, depending on the contractor. Peto insisted on weekly pay, but elsewhere monthly pay was more usual and sometimes when a contract was going badly, the men were not paid at all if the sub-contractor absconded. A new man coming on the job could not wait a month for his pay, so he took advances in credit tickets, was short of cash by the first pay day and remained in debt often until the contract was completed. Cash received on pay day was too often spent on drink, the 'randies' often lasting for several days until the money ran out. Fights between Irish and Scots, Scots and English or labourers on different contracts broke out at such times, terrifying the locals, who must have been heartily thankful when the railway was completed.

Little accommodation was available in the cramped cottages of English villages. Even when it was, fathers were fearful for their daughters and did not wish their sons to go off with the navvy gangs, so the two groups tended to keep their distance from each other. Decent lodgings also cost money, so it was easier and cheaper to build a shanty from whatever was locally available – stone in rocky parts, turf in the mosses and fenlands, branches, leaves, whatever came to hand. Those who did not make their own hovel often dossed down in another's, taking it in turns to sleep in the cramped confines while a partner worked.

Under such conditions, with food cooked over open fires,

working in all weathers with insufficient protection, having no warm, dry home to which to return, the prevalence of disease was not surprising. In the worst circumstances 'they lived like brutes, they were depraved, degraded and reckless. Drunkenness and dissoluteness of morals prevailed. There were many women but few wives; loathsome forms of disease were universal. Work often went on without intermission on Sundays as well as on other days.' In the eyes of the clergy, the last sin was probably the greatest of all the navvies' faults.

There is no doubt, from the number of complaints of such camps that they were common in the early days of railway contracting. The small contractors themselves had often been bred in such a system and could see no reason for altering what had given them their own start, but it became a nationwide scandal and at least some of the contractors did something to alleviate the squalor, mental and physical. Mr Jackson, a large railway contractor, found that 'setting aside any reference to feeling as to the comfort and condition of the men, and looking at it from a business point of view, that it is much more profitable, much more comfortable, and much better in every respect that the men should be taken care of'. By erecting over sixty wooden cottages and looking after the morals of the men in his employ, a useful start was made in curbing the worse abuses of a system that had grown too large for traditional methods.

The navvy was wanted only as long as his strength remained. The way of life that had developed on railway sites meant that at the end of a contract the navvy was 'discharged penniless, and has returned discontented, reckless, deteriorated in bodily and mental condition, or he has, with others of the same class, entered the ranks of able-bodied mendicants, vagrants and depredators, of whom the committals within the last few years have been so largely increased'.[7]

The first great wave of railway building subsided in the early 1840s when a trade depression led to many bankruptcies and few new proposals for railways. New reputations had been established for young engineers such as Locke and Brunel, for contractors such as Peto and Brassey. The beginnings of a national system of railways were on the ground and operating.

Once trade recovered from the depression, the second Railway
Mania eclipsed anything hitherto seen in its demand for the
services of contractors and engineers. Meanwhile the survivors
of the first round completed contracts and Brassey showed the
Continent of Europe what had been achieved in a hectic half a
decade of trial and error. One engineer and one contractor could
now be made responsible for constructing a whole railway. It was
a tremendous step forward.

3
Boom and Bust

More British railways were promoted in the period between 1844 and 1847 than ever before or since. It was such a great surge of investment that the name given to the period, the second Railway Mania, has stuck ever since. Lines sanctioned at that time were still being built into the early 1850s, while many were never built at all, as some of the proposals were over-ambitious or merely fraudulent.

Immediately before the second Railway Mania there were 2,235 miles of railway route in operation. The North, the Midlands and the London area, as well as the Central Lowlands of Scotland were reasonably well provided. However, Wales, the remainder of Scotland, East Anglia and the West Country were left singularly lacking in the new mode of transport. In 1844 nearly 1,000 miles of railway were authorised but unbuilt, including the main line from London to Norwich and Yarmouth. Hopes were extravagantly high, as the following suggests: 'The idea of a grand railway route through the Eastern Counties of England to the port of Yarmouth, which thus linked to the Metropolis was to distance even Liverpool in its fabulous increase in prosperity, was one of the schemes of 1835'.[1]

At a time when the main impetus to build railways came from promoters and their ability to raise capital for construction, it required favourable economic conditions to launch major railway projects. The depression of the early 1840s was replaced in 1844 by a marked quickening of the economy and a rash of new railway schemes was put forward. Nearly 3,000 miles of route were sanctioned in the one year of 1845. Enormous though that figure was, greater than all the route mileage constructed up to that time, the following year brought forth 270 railway Acts for the construction of a further 4,540 miles of railway, a figure which subsided to a mere 1,415 miles in 1847 when the bubble of promotions was pricked by one of the recurrent financial panics that gripped Victorian England, seemingly in every decade.

Nearly 9,000 miles of railway route had been sanctioned by Parliament in a hectic three-year period during which stock market speculation had reached fever pitch. In the event only 5,000 of these miles were actually constructed up to 1852. Even so, this more than tripled the national railway mileage in a mere seven years. It was the peak of British railway construction, giving contractors their busiest period ever. Fortunately they were better prepared than they had been in the 1830s, but the sheer volume of work brought other problems hitherto unanticipated. At the same time, the state of the financial markets proved a grave source of continuing anxiety for contractors and railway directors alike.

Contracting methods were still largely manual, so that an increase in the work-load automatically meant a proportional increase in the labour force. The organisation of works still largely depended on the abilities of the engineer, architect and contractor, but now they had to rely much more on their agents as the sheer quantity of work precluded personal supervision on a day-to-day basis. By the mid-1840s there was a body of able contractors in existence. The previous Railway Mania and subsequent depression had winnowed out the inadequates to a considerable degree, so that the necessary dilution of talents inherent in the vast expansion of construction was from a relatively sound base of tried and capable men, but the sheer volume of the new work meant that:

> Contractors there were, doubtless, whom railways brought only like bubbles to the surface in order that they might burst and be got rid of. There were some who, moderately successful in small contracts, failed utterly in the fulfilment of large ones. There were others who thought they were safe in undertaking vast works where they imagined they would not be very closely overlooked, hoping to puzzle inspection by the extent and intricacy of their labours; but who soon found to their confusion that the subtlety of their tricks, even when dispersed over hundreds of miles, was quite matched by the subtlety of Mr. Locke's investigation. These usually denominated scamping contractors, spent the remainder of their time in abusing the engineer whom they had been unable to dupe.[2]

The whirlwind of Railway Mania promotions highlighted the problems of railway contracting and engineering. The well-established engineer Sir John Rennie wrote about the profession in the mid-1840s:

> It was not the question of whether they were educated for it, or competent to undertake it, but simply whether any person chose to dub himself engineer; hence lawyers' clerks, surgeons, apprentices, merchants, tradesmen, officers in the army and navy, private gentlemen, left their professions and became engineers; the consequence was that innumerable blunders were made, vast sums of money were recklessly expended and the greater part of lines were thrown out of Parliament in consequence of the innumerable errors committed in them.[3]

The vastly inflated engineering profession was cut down to size again in the slump that followed the boom. Experienced bankers were unwilling to back unknown engineers or inexperienced contractors, so that the services of the competent minority were greatly sought by the most credit-worthy and soundly based of the projected railway companies. It was a case of the good seeking the good. Brassey was well connected financially with George Carr Glyn, banker to the mighty LNWR. On the continent, his banker was Edmund Blount of Paris. Peto's East Anglian connections with the Gurney banking family of Norwich stood him in good stead in times of crisis. Their standing with reputable bankers enabled them to maintain their cash flow when income was irregular. It also reassured their suppliers, who could thus be reasonably certain of future payments from sound contractors and could themselves raise loans against bills drawn by those contractors. Discounted bills maintained the forward momentum of contracts at several critical points during the fraught years of the late 1840s.

Those who dealt with lesser contractors had a number of unpleasant experiences, including even Sir John Rennie 'from taking on dubious work . . . before I could balance my accounts, most of the companies had vanished, remaining largely in my debt'.[4]

The greatest of the contractors are the subject of later chapters, but it as well to remember that about half the lines built between

1844 and 1866 were constructed by smaller contracting companies whose names are largely unknown outside the minute books of the railways for whom they worked. As with the engineers and surveyors already noted, great expansion brought forward many incompetents, the subject of abuse by many contemporary writers. The two trans-Pennine railways from Manchester to Leeds and Sheffield suffered particularly from contracts with large numbers of contractors of varying abilities. Railways such as these continued the 1830s system of dividing the line to be built into short sections and then advertising for contractors locally. While this worked reasonably well in districts with a long history of canal and mining contracts, the further the sites were from established industrial areas the greater the problems. The boom precipitated an influx of labour from peripheral parts of the British Isles. They came together in large groups, under the nominal control of a ganger, each group often incomprehensible to other groups from other parts of the country. The ganger was responsible to the contractor, but in the absence of legal contracts, this was often difficult to maintain.

Abuses bred under such a loose system of control. The second Railway Mania was a period of notorious flouting of such laws as there were to protect employees. The Truck Act was widely disregarded despite remonstrances from the engineers in charge. The housing, health and safety of the navvies was scandalously ignored by many of the lesser contractors and by several of the major ones. The result was that a Select Committee was set up to hear evidence of abuses. Of the contractors who gave evidence, only Peto and Dargan came out well under the spotlight of an official enquiry. Fortunately for the work-force matters improved after the Mania period. Fewer contractors meant that the worst contractors were winnowed out.

The 'tommy shop' was a feature on many contracting sites. The goods were not of the highest quality or lowest price: 'oatmeal is about 1d a peck more, and not so good as at the other shops'. The other vital constituent of the navvies' diet, bread, was of 'deficient weight. The quality of some of the articles is exceedingly bad, the tea and butter, and those things.' The tommy shop sold loaves obtainable elsewhere at 8d for 10d, 5s

worth of tea at 8s and so on. The original logic of delaying
payment had been that the men would go on a drinking spree
once they had the money, so the fewer times they were paid the
better. However, William Jackson, contractor to the L&BR and
later a partner of Brassey, confessed that 'the longer payments
are delayed the greater the chances are of excesses being
committed by many of the men'. A final word on the subject
came from Mr Deacon, himself a sub-contractor and a former
truck-shop keeper, who stated that he preferred weekly payments
as he got the labour better done and better men for his money.
Yet the abuses continued.

Housing of the work-force had hardly improved since the early
days. Twenty huts on the South Devon Railway housed between
150 and 200 men, the remainder making themselves mud and
turf huts with a tiny window, 12ft square being the average size.
On the Hawick contract of the North British Railway, the local
contractor built huts which he rented out to keepers, who in turn
charged 1s to 1s 6d a week for the use of a bunk, two and three
men using each bunk; a dozen bunks filled a room the size of a
drawing-room, and the hut was built up against the hillside from
turf, running with water in winter and no internal divisions to
give privacy. Others lodged in villages when possible. In
Lockerbie, six or seven slept in one room; exceptionally a two-
roomed house had no less than twenty-one people sleeping there.
Others took up with local girls, abandoning them when they
moved on.

One solution offered to the squalor came from Peter
Thompson, a contractor and builder, who designed a cheaply
built and sparsely furnished but reasonable 'labourers' moral
cottage'. The morality referred to the fact that there were
internal walls to keep the sexes apart. With fixtures and fittings it
was to cost no more than £65 and could be moved from site to
site. There were few takers.

By far the worst aspect revealed of contracting work in the
second Railway Mania was that of the death and injury of
labourers both at work and in their squalid encampments. They
were being driven on at a pace unknown in the past. The
Woodhead tunnel on the Sheffield & Manchester Railway was

"LABOURERS' MORAL COTTAGE."

Elevation

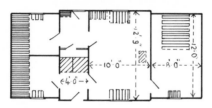

Plan of Cottage, showing the Fittings

THE ARRANGEMENT OF PLAN AS FOLLOW: –

Entrance Lobby	6 ft. 3 in. by 4 ft
Living Room	12 ft. 8 in. by 10 ft
Parents' Bed Room	12 ft. 0 in. by 8 ft
Back Lobby	6 ft. 3 in. by 4 ft
Girls' Bed Room	8 ft. 0 in. by 6 ft
Boys Bed Room	8 ft. 0 in. by 6 ft

Price of Cottage, from £40 to £50, according to locality; are built stud framed, either brick nog, plaster in cement, or lath plaster cement to outside; and boarded, canvassed, and paper inside; slate, tile, or asphalted felt roof; wood floor throughout; except the lobbies, paved with brick; ceiling plastered; glazed iron casements and fastenings; doors with proper fastenings; wood stained oak colour.

The price of the fittings and fixtures from £12 to £15 as follow:

TO ENTRANCE LOBBY. – A place for fuel, rail, and pins.

TO LIVING ROOM. – Cooking stove, open fire, an oven, &c.; a dresser with drawer, shelves over, and potboard under, 2 bracket tables.

TO BED ROOMS. – Three iron bedsteads, 3 mattresses, 3 bolsters, 3 bracket tables, 2 wardrobes with shelves.

TO BACK LOBBY. – Sink with waste pipe, a pantry with shelves, &c., rails and pins to bed rooms.

An ideal of housing rarely achieved in early railway construction the scene of some of the most frequent and long-lasting problems of this kind. The surgeon to the line, H. L. Pomfret, gave details to the Statistical Society of Manchester and later to the Select Committee on accidents at the site. There were

> 23 cases of compound fractures, including two cases of fractured skull. 74 simple fractures, including two fractures of scapula, three fractures of clavicle, one fracture of patella, one fracture of astragalus, 140 severe cases, including burns from blasts, severe contusions, lacerations, dislocations, etc; one man lost both his eyes and one half his foot. Most of these accidents were connected with other injuries; for instance, a man had his arm broken by a blast, the limb was much burned, together with one eye and much of the side of the head and face; there were several cases of broken ribs also among these cases; there have also been 450 cases of minor accidents, including trapped and broken fingers, injuries to feet and toes, lacerations of the scalp etc., bruises, broken shins etc. In five of these cases the fingers required amputation; many of these minor accidents were occasioned by drinking and fighting.[5]

This line became notorious, one of the contractors, Thomas Nicholson, feeling constrained to write a pamphlet in his own defence. But so little had been done to alleviate the misery of the navvy encampments on the moors above Sheffield that there were outbreaks of disease, including cholera. Certainly there was much carelessness and drunkenness on the part of the navvies themselves. Their use of iron stemmers to ram home explosive charges caused many premature explosions by striking sparks, which the use of more expensive and softer copper stemmers would have prevented. The habit of the men riding on tip wagons was another frequent cause of crushed limbs. Ropes broke, barrows overturned, earth slipped, but above all there was a lack of effort to prevent accidents on the part of the contractors and their underlings. When hospital treatment was given after an accident it was rarely the contractor who paid. Northampton Infirmary, close to the London & Birmingham Railway, had 124 cases from the railway, for which expenditure was £590. Only £15 1s 0d of this was contributed by the contractor. At Salisbury, while Brassey was building the western extension of the London & South Western Railway, fifty-two cases were admitted, only £6 6s 0d of whose costs were paid by the contractor. Casualties were much lighter on the Southampton & Dorchester Railway, but nevertheless there were seven fatalities and some ten or more serious injuries. The lack of

> precautionary arrangement, of improved instruments or methods of working, the recourse to which lies entirely in the power of the employer . . . where the want of skill, or the imprudence of one man, may endanger the safety of several fellow workmen, the correction of such a source of risk seems, as fully, to lie within the means of the employer, as the precaution against accident arising from imperfect tools, or ill-constructed machinery.[6]

Already in the 1840s workers in factories were protected from the negligence of their employers, but on construction sites and in coal mines accidents continued to multiply until renewed depression cut down the numbers at work and thereby the number of accidents.

At the peak of the second Railway Mania there were some 249,000 men employed in the construction of railways. By far the largest employers were Brassey, Peto and Dargan in Ireland who together accounted for nearly half of the lines built between 1844 and 1852. Peto and Dargan in particular tried to improve the welfare of their men; Brassey and his partners did so to a lesser extent. The other half of the contracting picture was much blacker. Smaller men out to make their fortune quickly appear to have been less than anxious to curb abuses. Responsibility could be easily shed by blaming the sub-contractor or ganger. The injured labourer would be cast off, often without compensation, with only a few shillings in his pocket collected by his mates.

That there were faults on both sides is evident from contemporary press reports:

Yorkshire Gazette, June 6 1849
DRIFFIELD – AFFRAY WITH NAVVIES
The navies[sic] employed on the works of the Burdale Tunnel on the Malton & Driffield Railway were lately discharged in consequence of the suspension of the works. These desperadoes having been turned loose on the world, commenced killing game, and whatever else came in their way. On the nearest farm, occupied by Messrs Acklam, is a rabbit warren, which, of course, did not escape the marauding incursions of the navvies. One night, Messrs Acklam, with some of their men, proceeded to the warren to observe what the navvies might

be after, when, between 40 and 50 ruffians, armed with guns and clubs, rushed upon them, and swore they would murder Messrs Acklam and their men. Mr Samuel Acklam was felled to the ground with a blow from the butt end of a gun, and whilst down was severely kicked and beaten. One of the navvies named Spigo, having come up, and found that it was Mr Samuel Acklam, swore he would blow out the brains of any man that injured him, for he was a good fellow. Had not this man interfered, Mr Acklam would most likely have been left dead in the field. He was dreadfully wounded and his life was despaired of, but he is now out of danger. They also turned Mr Acklam's cattle out of the fold yard, and caused damages to the amount of £10 at the least. Messrs Acklam have been very kind to the men the whole time that they have been employed on the line.

Yorkshire Gazette, 29 April 1848
RIOT AT MARKET WEIGHTON

On Thursday four navigators were brought before the magistrates at Market Weighton charged with a riot. On the previous Tuesday the defendants and about 50 other Englishmen were working on the railway in the neighbourhood of the above town along with a number of Irishmen. The latter were employed in getting ballast, and the English labourers, imagining that the Irish were working for lower wages than themselves, went to Mr Calvert the contractor, insisting upon their dismissal. Mr Calvert, however, refused to comply with their demands, whereupon a large party of the English attacked the Irish, who retreated, and three of them took shelter in the house of James McGrath, a shop and lodging house keeper in Market Weighton. Mrs McGrath seeing the mob following, shut the door, and immediately afterwards the men came up, some armed with large sticks, and endeavoured to force an entrance. The Police were called and caused the crowd to disperse.

The gangs of men whom the contractors recruited were not often detailed in early written records, but Prof Patmore has traced the composition of one such gang from census and other records. They were working on the East & West Ridings Junction Railway from Starbeck to York via Knaresborough during the census of 1851. The ages of the gang ranged mostly from 15 to 44 years of age with the biggest group in the 25 to 29 age group. There were a few in the 50 to 54 age group who were probably foremen.

A quarter of the work-force came from within a dozen miles of Knaresborough while many more were from nearby parts of

Joseph Firbank

Sir Joseph Thomas Firbank, MP,
Joseph Firbank's son

Thomas Brassey

William Fairbairn

William Dargan, builder of
most of Ireland's major railways

Weetman Pearson,
later Lord Cowdray

Sir Charles Fox

Sir Douglas Fox

Yorkshire. Other English elements came from Lincolnshire which provided a large contingent and there was a scattering from most English counties, but none came from Wales. The largest single contingent was the 26 per cent of the work-force from Ireland, always a common source of navvy gangs in the north of England.

While the line was being built, many in the work-force lodged in Knaresborough and went to the diggings daily, so that at the peak of construction a tenth of the Knaresborough labour force was described as being railway labourers. Such a great increase put an enormous strain on already inadequate accommodation. A single cottage usually housing an agricultural labourer and four children was, in 1851, at bursting point with an additional nineteen lodgers, including four married couples and three children. The Irish labourers tended to occupy separate quarters. An Irish widow in the town who already had two daughters managed to squeeze seventeen lodgers into the house, including three married couples and ten children. All this overcrowding was in the already cramped, poorer part of the town, thus making a serious situation critical.[7]

By the late 1840s the greatest railway contractors were national figures by reason of their wealth, the huge labour forces that they commanded and the power that they wielded, both as a result of their purchasing power in industry and of their entry into national politics. Despite the onset of financial crisis in the autumn of 1847, most of the works then sanctioned were continued. Brassey tided the hard-pressed Great Northern Railway over a difficult patch in 1848 by accepting mortgage bonds in lieu of cash, and later aided the North Staffordshire Railway in the same way. He and his greatest contemporaries consorted with leading bankers, British and foreign: Baring, Rothschild, Gurney and Blount were but a few of those who secured the finances of contractors. They were major customers of the great ironmasters, engineering firms, timber importers, quarry owners and brickmakers who all saw the contractors as sources of large orders and profits.

'Having completed as they consider their work at home, they have started on a kind of knight-errantry to supply railway

deficiencies all over the world.' At the end of the great
constructional period which supplied Britain with almost all its
important main lines, the words of the *Railway Times* in 1852
may have seemed true at the time, but in the following twenty
years the mileage of the British system more than doubled, so
that although the pace was slower than at the height of the
second Railway Mania, building had by no means ceased. The
waggons, rails, tools and, above all, the labour force that the
contractors had gathered in the period of fast expansion, had to
seek new outlets. Doubtless the richest contractors could have
retired to enjoy their fortunes, but they were not made that way.
They were constantly seeking new horizons for the expertise and
capital that they had so painfully gathered by trial and error in
the heroic period. If local people would not promote enough
railway mileage to keep them busy, they could do the job
themselves. If opportunity were lacking at home, then there was
more than enough across the seas.

By 1850 the contractors were national figures who supported
the Great Exhibition, were sought after to grace the dinner tables
of the establishment and had the ear of anybody who was some-
body in the national hierarchy. Presentation to royalty was but a
little way off. Their mansions were featured in the *Illustrated
London News*, their after-dinner remarks printed in *The Times*.
In a word, they had arrived.

By 1852 the only places of some importance not connected by
rail to the rest of the country were Inverness and Hereford. Mid-
Wales, Galloway, the Scottish Highlands and much of western
Ireland were without rail communication, but they could not
boast a single town larger than a modern small market town.
Thus the scope for further expansion of the British railway
system must have appeared limited to conservative contemporaries of the great contractors. Yet many of the existing routes
were circuitous. For instance, London to Margate via Redhill
and Ashford, or Cardiff to Merseyside via Gloucester and Crewe
seemed open invitations to cut-off routes. New mineral
discoveries also tempted railway promotion ever deeper into the
South Wales valleys or across the Pennines to link the ores of
Furness with the furnaces of Teesside. A third source of new

promotion was the development of new resorts and industries, ports and suburbs. The benefits of economic shock therapy administered by the railways to sleepy Southampton and yawning Yarmouth had already been noted by Peto. Finally, many settlements that had rejected or been missed by the original railways were now loudly demanding branch lines to serve them. It was on these premises that a new round of railway promotion started in the glow of economic self-satisfaction generated by the success of the Great Exhibition.

Although Peto, Brassey, Betts and Wythes were the names that cropped up time and again in relation to railway contracts, they were far from being the only contractors active after the collapse of the second Railway Mania. Sir Charles Fox, later mentioned in connection with Queensland, did his contracting work through his firm of Fox, Henderson & Co which was occupied in the early stages of the London, Chatham & Dover Railway in association with Thomas Russell Crampton, locomotive engineer and contractor, and George Burge, developer of Herne Bay, who between them took £90,000 of shares in the original subscription list. Two firms with both home and overseas interests were Waring Brothers, who built much of the Somerset & Devon Railway, the western sections of the future Midland & Great Northern Joint Railway and parts of the Midland Railway, as well as sections of Portuguese railways; also growing fast in the late 1850s was the firm of Messrs Smith & Knight, involved abroad in Sardinia and Mexico at an unfortunate time, but chiefly remembered as the contractors of the first section of the Metropolitan Railway from Paddington to Farringdon.

Thomas Crampton and William Buddicom were interesting examples of the range of abilities found in some early contractors. They were born within a few weeks of each other in 1816. Crampton was trained as a locomotive engineer under Daniel Gooch, Buddicom as a builder's apprentice. Crampton's name lives on mainly as the designer of a popular single-driver express engine, more appreciated on the Continent than at home. His contracting work in Kent, eastern Europe and Asia Minor was supplemented by laying the Anglo-French submarine cable and inventing a chalk slurrying machine intended for the

Channel tunnel. Buddicom was, if anything, even more versatile. After work with Locke on the L&MR and the GJR, he was appointed locomotive superintendent of the latter railway at the age of 24. He then proceeded to transfer the works from Edge Hill to Crewe, designed the 'Crewe' type locomotive, and in 1841 was to be found in France with Brassey and Locke setting up the great Sotteville works at Rouen and contracting to run the Paris & Rouen Railway and its extensions. Many other lines in France were supplied with engines and rolling stock from Sotteville. He later contracted to build the difficult Lyons & Geneva Railway and other lines in France and Italy, before retiring to the life of a country gentleman in North Wales in 1870. He was one of the few contractors to have a comfortable and lengthy retirement.

During the 1850s the contractors had by and large reversed their original role. Whereas in the 1830s and 1840s they had tendered for the contracts advertised by railways and engineers, or been persuaded to take on a contract by an engineer who thought them reliable, they now increasingly promoted, financed and generally encouraged the building of railways, sometimes doing the whole job themselves from start to finish with the aid of local nominees. Overseas they could go straight to the heads of government to seek concessions, suggesting means of finance from land grants, government stocks, sales of shares or variations thereon. Count Cavour in Italy, Prince Couza in Rumania and Prince Albert in Britain were all helped by contractors with railway and exhibition schemes, negotiating with them personally. Most commercial, manufacturing and shipping organisations, banking and insurance companies became more and more involved with contracting as the new network spread worldwide. Knighthoods were bestowed on Peto and Jackson, who were both MPs as well, while Dargan and Brassey could decline such marks of social distinction without offending royalty.

The system of railways that had evolved by the early 1860s already had much duplicate mileage between major and even some minor centres. None of the planning exercised in Belgium and France was evident in the jumble of routes that was emerging in Britain. Contractors pressed on to fill obvious gaps like central Wales and the remoter parts of Scotland, seemingly regardless of likely lack of traffic. Elsewhere, new routes between existing railway centres were being spawned ever more rapidly in the early 1860s, while a new type of financing was growing to support the designs of the contractors, which involved finance companies advancing money in return for shares and of the issuing of bonds of dubious value.

The majority of railways were built by contractors rather than by direct labour, and in the period 1844 to 1866, half of them by the great contractors of the day. These men provided a service that was superior to that of the 1830s, but even so railway managements seem to have had nagging doubts about the size of contracting profits, probably thinking that the jobs could have been done more cheaply by railway management using either direct labour or by letting out the works to directly controlled sub-contractors. The very obvious wealth of the great men in railway contracting indicated that profits could be enormous, but then so were the risks.

Building and operating contracts were commonplace, but so also were maintenance contracts in the early days of railways. One such between the London & North Western Railway and Richard Madigan of Hampstead Road, St Pancras was to supply locomotives, tools, wagons and materials between Watford, Leighton Buzzard and the Hillmorton ballast pits. He also had to clear debris from the Tring and Blisworth cuttings, where rockfalls were a hazard to traffic. The contract lasted for three years and one month from 31 May 1848. It included detailed prohibitions against Sunday work, unless absolutely necessary, a ban on trading by the contractor and a detailed list of fines to which Madigan was subject should he disobey the vast array of detailed rules drawn up by the company solicitor. Richard Madigan signed the contract with a strong, literate signature, unlike many of his lesser contemporaries.

The lengthy contract document gives a fascinating sidelight on the large amount of equipment needed by a contractor less than two decades after the opening of the first main-line railway. The total agreed valuation of Madigan's stock in trade was £33,134 17s 7d. The 155 wheelbarrows for ballast were valued at £115 5s

0d and the 3in wheeling planks on which they worked numbered 4,010, costing £83 10s 10d, and so on down to a pick-shaft at 6d and a ¼ gallon tin funnell (sic) at a mere 3d. The largest item was wagon stock at £14,083 10s 0d, while erection of wagon shop, wheel store, smith's shop, engine shop and fitters' shop, office, and the furniture and tools for them, added greatly to costs. There were also eleven locomotives, all small tender engines:

Number	Name		Value
1	Victoria	engine & tender	£700
2	Wharncliffe	,,	£1200
3	Blisworth	,,	£700
4	Brockhall	,,	£800
5	Contractor	,,	£1200
6	Leeds	,,	£1150
7	Camden	,,	£1250
8	Albert	,,	£750
9	Bury	,,	£950
10	Firefly	,,	£400
–	Hercules	,,	£350

Creditworthy railway companies had good access to both finance and materials. They were by far the largest firms regularly employing labour and had the largest body of trained managers in the country. In terms of capital the LNWR was thirty times the size of the largest manufacturing company in the 1850s, and over five times the size of the Brassey organisation at its peak. Despite such a concentration of resources, the railway companies had very mixed experiences when they tried to do work normally undertaken by contractors. The bureaucratic nature of the great railway was the antithesis of the personal contact and quick decision-making that typified the contractors and their trusted agents. It was also generally assumed that contractors were more capable than gentlemanly managers of getting hard graft from the navvies. The later example of moderately successful use of direct construction by the Eastern & Midlands Railway seems to point to smaller railways having greater success in this field than a major railway. To take another example from East Anglia, the Great Eastern Railway attempted a direct-labour contract when making the East Norfolk Railway from North Walsham to Cromer, with control emanating from

Liverpool Street. It was not a success and the company immediately reverted to normal contracting methods for the remaining sections of the line.

4

The Contracting Giants

For a quarter of a century, from 1840 until 1866, the names of Brassey, Peto and Betts were at the forefront of railway contracting worldwide as well as in Britain. Their involvement started as builders of sections of railways, but they rapidly became involved in the planning, promotion, financing and running of numerous railways, owning a number of subsidiary enterprises such as engineering works, brickyards and quarries, docks and shipping, hotels and property development, public utilities and insurance. Yet the contractors were not multinational corporations, nor even a limited company, but a loose partnership with a variety of other partners and agents, constantly dissolving and reforming in new guises. The trio of great men managed up to a third of all British railway construction, together with vast overseas and non-railway interests with only primitive single-contract accounts and complete trust in their agents to guide them.

Just how remarkable the position of the contracting giants was can be judged from their importance in the economy of Britain alone. In the peak year of railway construction, 1847, they employed nearly 2 per cent of the country's work-force, used about 10 per cent of the iron produced for home consumption and probably similar quantities of stone, bricks and other structural materials. Their overseas projects were at times on an even more gigantic scale, largely using British materials and much British labour. At its peak, the partnership between the three men was the largest single employer in Britain, appeared to have a larger cash flow than even the mighty LNWR (the world's largest company in 1847) and was the largest single customer of British industry. It was fortunate that so much power was in such generally competent hands in the period often regarded as Britain's economic golden age.

The man who was later to partner Brassey in his greatest joint projects worked independently of him during the second Railway Mania. Samuel Morton Peto had commenced his contracting partnership with his cousin, Thomas Grissell, in 1830, when they jointly inherited the business of their uncle, Henry Peto, at whose works he was apprenticed. He learned every aspect of the trade by practical experience and was able to lay 800 bricks a day. Peto and Grissell's first railway work, building the two Curzon Street stations in Birmingham, was followed by a contract for the Hanwell and Langley section of the Great Western Railway, which included the controversial Wharncliffe Viaduct. Work on the Yarmouth & Norwich Railway and the South Eastern Railway occupied Peto during the depression years, greatly increasing his mastery of the problems of varied railway construction. When contracts started to flow freely again in 1844, Grissell and Peto were able to bid for great mileages in the sure knowledge that they could complete them in good time. They concentrated on the eastern counties, completing the line from London to Norwich, then constructing the branch from Ely to Peterborough, all in record time, as well as filling in with branches from Wymondham to Dereham and from March to St Ives. The completion of the Norfolk Railway from Reedham to Lowestoft and his purchase of the harbour and waterways there gave him the base from which he launched his plans to make Lowestoft a major port. He bought a house to match his new status in life, Somerleyton Hall, which he had reconstructed to his own taste by Charles Henry Lucas, his agent for the Norwich & Brandon Railway, who was himself to become one of the greatest railway contractors in his own right.

Thomas Grissell tired of the strenuous life of a railway contractor so it was agreed that the partnership should be split. Peto took over all railway operations, while cousin Thomas continued for three years after the dissolution of the partnership was made final in 1846 with the construction of the Houses of Parliament and the completion of other unfinished civil contracts. He thus followed David McIntosh (a contemporary contractor) into early retirement. The new partner for Peto was Edward Ladd Betts, who started his contracting career on the

Grand Junction Railway under George Stephenson, for whom he built Dutton Viaduct. Although not in partnership with Peto at the time, they together built most of the South Eastern Railway, having adjoining contracts. He also performed much work in the Chester area, including part of the Chester & Holyhead Railway as well as branches to Mold and to Wrexham. The first fruit of the joint endeavours of the new firm of Messrs Peto & Betts was the Great Northern Railway's line from Peterborough to Boston, Lincoln and Doncaster and its associated East Lincolnshire Railway from Boston to Louth. This was construction on as massive a scale as Brassey in this country. Their overseas contracts came in the following decade.

The size of contracts that the major firms were able to execute can be judged from the cost of construction. Wages in the middle of the nineteenth century were about one hundredth of their present-day nominal amount, so that the £36m of Brassey contracts in the 1840s and over £20m handled by Peto, Grissell and Betts in that decade represent some £5 billion in modern money. The largest contracting firms had undergone phenomenal expansion, so that the £420,000 contract that Peto took from the Southampton & Dorchester Railway in 1845 was by then small beer, but he nevertheless gave it close attention. He had started to do what was later to become commonplace, accept shares in lieu of cash, in this case a mere £25,000 which he could retain as an investment or dispose of later, hopefully at a profit once the line was fully operational and paying dividends. When there was trouble with the tunnel under Southampton or with the earthworks, Peto appeared personally to solve the problem with the engineer, Captain Moorsom. Although these problems caused an overrun of £184,000 on the original estimate, the line was still built cheaply at a cost of less than £10,000 a mile, less even than many Irish railways.

What particularly distinguished Peto's works from those of most other contractors was the general calm that prevailed, even on pay nights. Peto was a fervent Baptist who set high standards for himself and his men. Weekly wages were the rule with him, cash was prescribed so tommy shops were frowned on to the extent of taking legal action against sub-contractors who tried to start the system on their works. Even when working in isolated areas far from shops and markets, he got supplies to his men by sending his agent 'to the nearest market town, and say, "I shall be paying away £500 or £600 a week to the men, and it will be to your interest to take care that the men are well supplied"; he would go to Ely, Peterborough, Whittlesea [sic], and instigate the different parties to come with a good and abundant supply on Saturday afternoon. At one place I saw several butchers' carts loaded with meat, and the butchers' men crying out, "who wants a fine leg of mutton?" and there is great competition to supply the men. At Ely you would see 30 or 40 bakers' carts, all piled up with bread, going into the Fens on Saturday to supply my men'.[1]

Not only were the men paid regularly and their money spent at full value on good quality merchandise, but Peto did his best to ensure that they drank less and had at least some instruction. As the Select Committee of 1846 reported, 'wherever his men were gathered in numbers, there a large room arose, in which, when heavy rains obstructed the work, it was no unpicturesque sight to view the hard, athletic navigator listening with grave attention to some volume which, striking at once his reason and his fancy, kept him from drink and saved him from debauchery. Many a man, before his engagement with Mr Peto in utter ignorance of everything, has been taught to read at his master's expense.'

The methods worked as a rule. The Bishop of Ely, who was also a magistrate, commented on how little work the bench had to do while the railways were being built in the district. Peto was described as a man whose agents 'gave the men religious and school books for the education of themselves and their children; and thus showing them that education can civilise the mind, reform the habits, and elevate the understanding. Dr Stanley, the Dean who uttered these words, went on to note that 'not one labourer in the Norwich district had been guilty of misconduct that made him amenable to the law'. There could have been few other railway sites in the country of which it was said that 'the gin shops were left deserted, and the schools were full'.

Dr Stanley was referring to the Peto system working at its best. Another contrasting example came from a clergyman, the Rev R. Wilson, who was examined by the Parliamentary Select

Committee enquiring into conditions of railway labour in 1846, referred to the Norwich & Brandon line and the neighbouring Swaffham to Dereham railway, where there was non-payment of wages and the 'labourers on the railways are really so ill-treated'. He found monthly or longer periods between payments and brutal language used by gangers against the navvies when they asked for their rights. Even so, the support that the navvies gave Peto when he stood in Norwich for Parliament a little later was convincing evidence that he was an outstandingly good employer for the period.

During the years of depression, the major contractors had been active in a number of fields. Thomas Brassey had done most of his work in France, which followed logically from the construction of the London & Southampton Railway. Joseph Locke was invited to engineer the line from Paris to Rouen, and Brassey, in partnership with William McKenzie who had undercut Brassey's very first tender on the Grand Junction Railway, proceeded to build the line of 82 miles in two years, continuing the line to both Dieppe and to Le Havre. Some 5,000 British navvies were taken over to commence operations, their physique and appetite for work being far greater than that of locally recruited labour. The one great setback was the collapse of the great viaduct at Barentin, which Locke and Brassey rebuilt immediately at no extra cost to the railway. Work continued with the even greater length of line from Orleans to Bordeaux, some 294 miles, which was completed in 1847. Such a prodigious output did not deflect Locke and Brassey from tendering successfully for work in Britain. With Locke as the engineer and Brassey as contractor in conjunction with agents and partners, whole regions of Britain had railway systems built by this formidable pair.

Starting with the Lancaster & Carlisle Railway in 1844, they added the Windermere branch, much of the Caledonian line from Beattock northwards, the Scottish Central Railway, the Scottish Midland and the Clydesdale Junction lines, while in East Anglia Brassey and Locke planned and constructed most of the Eastern Union Railway which radiated from Ipswich. In addition Brassey worked with several other engineers simultaneously. With Robert Stephenson he constructed some 31 miles of the Chester & Holyhead Railway, having earlier made the line from Crewe to Chester, the Trent Valley cut-off line from Rugby to Stafford and much of the North Staffordshire Railway. With Henry Robertson and Rendel he constructed most of the line from Birkenhead to Hereford via Shrewsbury. The *pièce de résistance*, however, was the Great Northern main line from London to Peterborough on which he worked with Cubitt. In all he was credited with the construction of nearly 800 route miles between 1844 and 1852 in Britain alone, about half of it with Locke. Meanwhile he continued his contracts in France which were as extensive as those in Britain. Naturally he could not supervise this expanding perimeter of work all by himself. He had started a partnership with William McKenzie on the Paris & Rouen contract. As the contracts multiplied, his agents on the spot became ever more important.

Stephen Ballard became Brassey's agent for the section of the Great Northern main line from Huntingdon to Peterborough which crossed the Fens. He was brought into Brassey's organisation from another contract in the Fenland where he was resident engineer constructing the middle level main drain. As was his custom, once Brassey trusted an agent, he left him to complete the job, which Ballard did by constructing rafts of peat sandwiched with faggots. When these filled in the swampy ground, they were gradually consolidated and de-watered, eventually providing an excellent trackbed for one of the premier main lines to the north. Ballard continued to serve Brassey almost to Brassey's death. His other contracts were in Holland, where his fen experience was again useful, and on the Worcester to Hereford line where tunnels through the Pre-Cambrian rocks of the Malvern Hills gave him some of the toughest tunnelling to be found in England. His final contract with Brassey was the Midland Railway main line from Bedford to Radlett, finished in 1868.

On the important Lancaster & Carlisle contract, Brassey was partnered by John Stephenson and William McKenzie. His agent was James Falshaw who had been an agent and later an engineering assistant for thirteen years before working for

Brassey. He was agent for most of the lines built in the Scottish Midlands in the 1840s, going on to build the first section of the Highland Railway as a partner in 1853. From 1859 until 1867 Falshaw worked on his own account from Edinburgh, building the Berwickshire Railway and the Blaydon and Consett line of the North Eastern Railway. Meanwhile he had been made a director of the Scottish Central Railway and thereafter became a director and finally chairman of the North British Railway in his adopted city. Other associates of Brassey at this time included most of the engineers and contractors who were to dominate the railways during their construction. Brassey's excellent choice of colleagues was one of the most important reasons for his success.

The great contractors had rapidly acquired methods of dealing with their huge responsibilities. Partnership spread the risk, and trusted agents enabled several contracts to be undertaken simultaneously in widely scattered locations. Yet the man at the top still kept contact with all that was going on. Brassey's dealings with his sub-contractors give us the flavour of the detailed control that he exercised:

When Mr Brassey took any contract he let out portions of the work to sub-contractors. His way of dealing with them was this: he generally furnished all the materials, and all the plant. I find him on one occasion ordering as many as 2400 waggons from Messrs Ransome & May. The sub-contractors contracted for the manual labour alone. I find that the sub-contracts varied from £5000 to £25,000; and that the number of men employed on them would be from one to three hundred – the former being more common than the latter.

Mr Brasseys' mode of dealing with sub-contractors was of an unusual kind, and such as could not have been adopted except by a man who had great experience of all kinds in manual work, and who was also a very just man. They did not exactly contract with him but he appointed to them their work, telling them what price he should give for it. All the evidence I have before me shows that they were content to take the work at his price, and that they never questioned his accuracy.

Frequently the work appointed to the sub-contractor turned out to be of a more difficult nature than had been anticipated. He however could not desist from the work on that account, nor make any appeal in unity to his employer. He would wait until the time when Mr Brassey should come round to visit the works. This was generally once or twice a month.

He came walking along the line as usual, with a number of followers. If a cutting, taken to be clay, turned out after a very short time to be rock he looked round, counted the number of waggons at work, scanned the cutting, and took stock of the nature of the stuff. 'This is very hard', said he to the sub-contractor. 'Yes, it is a pretty deal harder than I bargained for'. 'What is your price for this cutting?' 'So much a yard sir.' 'If you say that your price is so much, it is quite clear that you do not do it for that. I am glad that you have persevered with it, but I shall not alter your price; it must remain as it is, but the rock must be measured for you twice; will that do for you?' 'Yes, very well indeed, and I am much obliged to you, sir.'[2]

Sub-contractors knew that they were assured of a fair deal, but the Brassey method went much further. He had many long-serving and trusted gangers and navvies who followed him from job to job. He remembered their names, recalling them years later when they met again, sometimes hundreds or thousands of miles from the previous meeting place.

In many ways, Brassey's sites in the 1840s were much less enlightened than Peto's. Monthly payment and tommy shops were common features on his contracts, although evening classes and religious instruction were laid on for the men at Lockerbie, one of the main centres of the Caledonian contract. The clerk of the peace in that village testified that 'monthly payments had been attended with . . . great disorder; constant scenes of drunkenness, riot and all sorts of disturbance . . . the occasion of great scandal to the inhabitants of a quiet Scotch village'. On the Trent Valley contract there were loud complaints from the men against the truck system (tommy shops) operated by the sub-contractors, as there were on the Caledonian contract. There seemed to be much less control of the sub-contractors in the field of labour relations than over their earth-moving and con-structional work.

The perennial lack of ready cash made the labourer prey to the ganger, who was often the only literate person in the group. He had a notebook in which he entered the number of hours worked and advances made against work done. When he issued tickets for use at the store, he stopped a penny in the shilling on the advance. It was alleged that the storekeeper then paid 7½ per cent to the ganger or sub-contractor on what he sold. Other deficiencies in treatment of navvies emerged during the giving of evidence at the Parliamentary Select Committee of 1846.

Mr Alexander Ramsey was examined in relation to the houses on the North British lines:

> 'You mentioned that these residences were unhealthy; have you any positive knowledge as to their being productive of sickness?'
>
> 'Yes, I have seen illness there; sore throats and bowel complaints constantly occurring; and small-pox, which is also very frequent.'
>
> 'More prevalent than elsewhere?'
>
> 'Yes, than in healthy and well-constructed dwellings; arising, as I believe from unhealthy sites and the imperfect construction of the buildings.'
>
> 'You would hardly call the dwellings of the labourers in Roxburghshire healthy?'
>
> 'I would say most of them are so.'
>
> 'These are more like Irish cabins, I suppose?'
>
> 'I have never been to Ireland; but in many of these places connected with the railways, a humane man would hardly put a pig into them.'
>
> 'Are the men employed on your works put in these places?'
>
> 'Yes; the huts are still occupied in that way.'[3]

The contractor on the Chester & Holyhead Railway, Edward Betts, employed scripture readers at his own expense 'to improve the physical, moral and religious condition of the labourers'. He was asked by Captain Moorsom at the Parliamentary Select Committee:

> 'Are you able to form any comparison between the state of those labourers subject to this system of instruction, and the ordinary condition of labourers employed where no such system is employed?'
>
> 'I think that hitherto it has not long enough been in operation to form a comparison. Some of the contractors are decidedly of the opinion that the effect has been to keep the men much more steady to their work, and quieter; there have been fewer disturbances.'[4]

The long period of domination of British railway contracting exercised by Peto, Brassey and Betts saw the building of most of the British railway network, many European, Indian and North American main lines and the beginnings of railways in Africa, Australia and South America. *Bradshaw's Railway Manuals* of the period are replete with the three names as contractors, directors, lessees and promoters of lines throughout the world. Their role changed from that of organisers of labour to

The Old Woodhead Tunnels on the Manchester, Sheffield & Lincolnshire Railway. The excavation of these tunnels caused many deaths and injuries in the 1840s (*from the collection of S.W.A. Newton and by permission of Leicestershire Museums, Art Galleries and Records Service*)

William Dargan's private saloon, as later used on the Midland Great Western Railway

Cut and cover contracting on the Metropolitan Railway in 1862, showing problems with pipes and massive timberwork

The construction of Kensington High Street Station on the Metropolitan District Railway in 1865. Although this station has been rebuilt, nearby Bayswater remains very similar (*London Transport Collection*)

controllers of national economies. Once the massive capital influx of the Railway Mania had run its course, the contractors became initiators of major schemes which promised work for labour, investment prospects for capital, orders for manufacturers and mineowners and links to the national railway system for more and more towns and villages. Bankers such as George Carr Glyn of London, the Hambros of Scandinavia, the Rothschilds of Paris and Frankfurt were familiars of the great contractors. Stocks and shares which the bankers accepted as collateral were disposed of on the Stock Exchange, making them amongst the biggest users of that institution.

The great contractors were the personification of big business in an age of great growth, before regulation curbed some of the larger-than-life aspects of their activities. Peto, Brassey and Betts were men who could meet the Stephensons, Locke and Brunel as equals. The multiplicity of their interests and appetite for work and travel was staggering, yet they continued thus for decades until the events of 1866 gave them pause and others came in to fill the vacuum that they left. A more detailed look at their methods and projects fills in the picture of the pioneering giants.

Lowestoft was the key point in a series of projects initiated by Peto and carried out with the help of Brassey. The port had been opened in 1831 to provide an alternative outlet for Norwich, which disliked its dependence on Yarmouth. A waterway known as the New Cut at Haddiscoe provided a direct link to the great city. The original scheme was a failure, bought up cheaply by Peto at the time that he constructed the Lowestoft branch of the Norfolk Railway and moved into Somerleyton Hall. He then built an outer harbour, making provision for a fast-growing fish trade that was loading over fifty railway wagons a day by 1855, bound for the rapidly growing markets of London and the Midlands. The *Norfolk Chronicle* in 1851 commented that 'the excellent accommodation and facilities afforded at our newly-erected fish-market for landing, packing and forwarding to all parts of the kingdom that perishable commodity, are now being availed of to a considerable extent by the Barking and other deep sea fishing smacks'. At the same time the enlarged port was also receiving the Northern Steam Packet Company's ships from

Tonning, then in Denmark. This service later linked directly with the Royal Danish Railway across the Jutland peninsula, with a branch deep into Schleswig, tapping the rich farmlands of the Baltic coast. The Danish system was built by Peto and Betts, but much more slowly than they had hoped, not yielding significant through traffic until the 1860s. The terms of the contract make interesting reading and are typical of several then in force:

254 – ROYAL DANISH. Established 1852–3. Royal concession, of a system of railways conceded to Messrs Peto and others, in perpetuity, with a guarantee against competition for 100 years. The present (or first) section consists of a line from Flensburg, extending southwards to Rendsburgh, mileage 69 English miles.

The line is under lease to the contractors, Messrs Peto and Betts under which contract it has been completed, and furnished with rolling stock and plant of every description at an expenditure on capital of £540,000. Guaranteed interest, six per cent; half surplus profits; term of lease, 14 years, terminable at 5 or 10 years, on notice by directors, on giving twelve months notice. The contractors give substantial security to the extent of £100,000. As any division of profits, beyond the six per cent guaranteed, can only be made yearly, the directors deem it unnecessary to submit details of revenue account till the first year of the lease shall have expired. Traffic necessarily limited at first, from opening of the line at the commencement of an unusually severe season, has shown symptoms of a steady increase since the beginning of spring, and since the public have become more alive to the advantages of this new mode of transit. The greatest impediment to an earlier development of the traffic has been the delay in the construction of the bridge across the Eyder forming the junction between the Royal Danish and Neuminster, which has arisen from circumstances beyond the control of the company or the lessees.[5]

However, there was still a considerable Danish trade through Lowestoft. An advertisement even encouraged farmers to visit Denmark to buy cattle and horses after the failure of feed in that country.

Lowestoft also had potential as a holiday resort. Its main disadvantage was the route to London via Norwich and Cambridge. The Eastern Union line from Ipswich to Norwich, now used by most trains, had been built in 1849, was but little used by the dog-in-the-manger Eastern Counties Railway. Peto planned his own connections from Lowestoft to its markets. Starting with a small local line from Haddiscoe to Halesworth, he developed the East Suffolk Railway, built jointly with Brassey. This linked Lowestoft to the Eastern Union Railway at Woodbridge and also had a branch from Yarmouth to Beccles, thus giving Yarmouth a much shorter main line to London. While the line was being built, Peto further proposed a line from Colchester to Maldon and Pitsea where it would join the London, Tilbury & Southend Railway, already built and leased by the redoubtable pair. Given running powers over the Eastern Union Railway from Woodbridge to Colchester, Peto would have achieved the construction of a third north–south main line in East Anglia, whose traffic he could doubtless have increased by expanding the role of Lowestoft, but it was not to be.

Problems arose from many quarters. The railway was to be parallel with an existing line only some 10–15 miles away, yet an 1855 estimate of the cost of the line from Haddiscoe to Woodbridge alone was £475,000. With double track and extensions to Lowestoft, Yarmouth, Framlingham, Snape and Leiston, a doubling of that sum was in prospect, yet this was but one of several dozen schemes in which Peto, Brassey and Betts were involved in the 1850s. There was some local support for the line from Richard Garrett, the Leiston engineer and some of the landowners, but it depended on the contractor to fill up the subscription list. The surly Eastern Counties Railway did not want competition for the already thin traffic, thus forcing Peto to promote the alternative line from Pitsea to Colchester at an estimated cost of £30,000 per mile for double track. Slow progress was made with the East Suffolk Railway. The ECR did not want it to carry through traffic abstracted from their system, so subscribers were reluctant to part with their money. Peto had also to fend off much criticism of a situation where a shareholder could say, 'there was a branch line to Sir Morton Peto's residence, it formed a straight line up to his gate and is 12 miles in length. It would be a dead loss to the shareholders and so would the Ipswich–Woodbridge line. It was not only the new Baronet's [Peto] park and house they were to consider but that he was the owner of a large part of Lowestoft.' To such criticism

Peto replied that the line passed through the garden of Suffolk and he would let the line stand or fall on its own merits. An example of another attack on him came in 1857 with the anonymous publication of a booklet entitled *Petovia*. It questioned his motives for building the line and cast doubt on the integrity of a plan that not only benefitted his Lowestoft investments but allowed him to build the line at a high cost per mile on figures set by an engineer frequently employed by him. The engineer in question, George Parker Bidder, was not a man to sully his name with dubious practices, and a valuation of the line was undertaken by no less an engineer than Robert Stephenson. But there was legitimate doubt about the propriety of contractors building their own lines, raising much of their own capital and making deals often to their own advantage. The East Suffolk Railway was eventually completed in 1859, by which time Peto had abandoned the idea of a Colchester–Pitsea link, in return for an arrangement with the Eastern Counties Railway to run the new railway, thus saving him further capital expenditure on locomotives and rolling stock.

Thomas Brassey was much more fortunate with one of his own independent ventures, the Portsmouth Direct Railway linking Havant with Guildford. Portsmouth was reached indirectly by the London & South Western Railway via Basingstoke and Winchester, while the London, Brighton & South Coast Railway ran trains via Redhill and Worthing. The Portsmouth Direct was a diagonal across a square of lines. Brassey promoted the Bill with the aid of local men in Guildford, Petersfield, Ryde, Portsmouth and Havant, the last being Admiral Sir James Stirling, but local subscribers could only be found for £40,220 of the estimated £305,920 cost of the line, while additional expenses brought the total capital and loan authority to £533,000. Joseph Locke and his partner John Errington were appointed engineers, building a single line with more curves and steep gradients than Locke would have thought proper, at least in his earlier days. The line was quite unashamedly built for sale to the highest bidder. The line fitted best the London & South Western Railway system, but the South Eastern Railway also had a line from London Bridge to Guildford via Redhill, while junction with the Brighton line at Havant provided a third possible customer. The Act for the line was obtained in 1853 but completion of the 32¼ mile line was not until 1859, thanks to the need to make deviations, troublesome earthworks in the clay and greensand belt traversed, the need to raise debentures in 1857 to complete the line and finally trouble with the LBSCR about making the junction at Havant. The line remained unsold until 1861, when the LSWR finally made the financially troubled line part of its own system. Such sagas of delay and difficult financing could be multiplied throughout the land in the 1850s. Railways were still wanted by many communities, but ability and willingness to pay for them was much more difficult than in the previous decade. Contractors had to devise schemes for over-coming this problem. Meanwhile, the major contractors built much more mileage overseas than they did at home. There was virgin territory to be broken in India, Australia and North as well as South America.

Most of the overseas contracts undertaken by British contractors in the 1850s and 1860s were executed by Brassey, Peto, Betts and other contractors partnering them or working alongside them. There were others, notably Waring Brothers and Smith & Knight, but their efforts pale beside those of the leading trio. Capital earned during the British Railway Mania became available for recirculation elsewhere. Further profits were reinvested as soon as they were made, the international connections of the bankers either pointing out where investment might be sought or actively encouraging the contractors to plan railways for them. The scope was literally worldwide. British industry was linked to sources of food and raw materials by the world's largest fleet of deep-sea vessels. Further increases in supplies necessitated the improvement of communications at the other end, which by 1850 could only be provided by rail in the absence of a navigable river. Work in France continued with the line from Lyons to Avignon, then in Italy, Spain and Austria-Hungary, where in the wake of the turbulence of 1848, the empire sought to have a rapid transit system capable of moving troops quickly to likely trouble spots. Even Norway had a Brassey & Peto railway from Christiania (Oslo) to Eidsvold, first section of the Norwegian Trunk Railway. They were both directors of the railway in its early years, together with the stockbroker J. L. Ricardo, MP.

Such activity would prostrate most people, but a further quotation shows a contemporary view of Thomas Brassey, and could as well have been applied to Peto: 'But time that brings slackened pace, and wealth that brings comparative love of leisurely ease to most men, have failed to stop or enervate Thomas Brassey. He is still the very Ashuerus of contractors. Men swear they have seen him at different places at times so little removed, that they doubt each other's accuracy. There is not a leading hotel in any leading town in continental Europe where letters are not lying for him. Today he is in Genoa; before the week is out he will be at Madrid. Seek him there, he has gone off to Russia. He knows no rest.'[6]

India was the scene of great railway building activity from 1853 onwards, especially after the Indian Mutiny of 1857 when, like Austria, the military benefits of a railway were realised after the event. A Brassey associate, George Wythes, was first on the scene, starting the Great Indian Peninsular Railway out of Bombay. The line was successful and profitable for the contractor, but the terms offered by the East India Railway of cost plus 10 per cent under the supervision of government engineers did not appeal to Brassey, who only started his extensive building there in the wake of the Mutiny. His least fortunate but most spectacular work was in Canada where the Grand Trunk Railway was promoted to link Quebec with Montreal, Toronto and Detroit. The promotion in 1852 had all the best credentials. It was supported by the colonial governments to the extent of £3m, and Robert Stephenson was appointed consultant engineer. Sir William Jackson, MP and contractor, had undertaken a survey with the company engineer, Alexander Ross, and bankers of no less esteem than Thomas Baring and George Carr Glyn had introduced the scheme to the investing public. The problems arose mainly through trying to build a railway to English standards in the raw pioneer lands of Canada and of making sure that the line and particularly the bridges stood up to the extremes of climate.

James Hodges, a former carpenter who had become a Brassey agent, was the contractor's man on the spot, while Betts was in charge of management. Brassey himself visited Canada to see the progress of the line. He sailed into New York where he had special cars attached to his trains so that he could view the country and its railways from the rear platform. He was a fêted personality, a legend even in the USA. The managers of the various railways travelled with him, valuing his presence and comments.

He was struck by the low cost of construction in the USA, where locally grown timber was used to make light trestle structures where he would have used bricks or masonry. The locomotives with their leading bogies and balloon stacks had to ride tracks that would soon have worn out the wheels of contemporary English engines, so violent was the vibration and oscillation set up, but to some extent smoothed by the bogies with their cast-iron wheels. The financing of railways by land grants of a belt of land a mile wide, was later to be used by him in a modified form in Argentina. Although the main criticism of the Grand Trunk Railway was its expensive and English nature, Brassey was very willing to learn from North American practice. He sent two of his mechanics to the USA to examine factories making rolling stock. The men were welcomed everywhere and were even supplied with drawings of the machines they inspected. They brought back planing and morticing machines for use by the organisation; such advanced products of Yankee labour-saving ingenuity were new to England. Likewise, steam excavators and a steam-driven bucket chain were used when labour was in short supply or the going was hard. Canadian labour cost 50 per cent more than the standard 5s per day of the English navvy, but only Anglo-Americans were found to be up to the mark in shifting 20 tons of spoil a day. The underfed French-Canadians 'except for very light work, were almost useless'.

A contemporary report indicated the enormous scale of operations, especially at Montreal, where the Victoria Bridge across the St Lawrence River was the centrepiece of the project:

In July 1853, Mr. Stephenson visited Canada for the express purpose of finally fixing the most eligible site and determining the dimensions and general character of the design; and having communicated his ideas to Mr Ross, who, in accordance with them, prepared and arranged all the information required, the result, in a very little time, was the adoption of the structure now far advanced to completion . . .

The contractors immediately engaged in preparing and procuring the extensive plant and machinery necessary for carrying on so large and formidable a work. Three steam-boats and forty barges, specially adapted for the duty to be performed, were immediately ordered to be constructed by the builders and manufacturers in the country. Arrangements were also made for machinery of various kinds used in such works, and ordered from England. Rafts of timber, as they floated down the St. Lawrence on their way to the usual emporium at Quebec, were stopped in their progress, and purchased for the use and construction of the coffer-dams necessary for getting in the foundations. Until the spring of 1854 these preparatory measures were in progress. Quarries for stone were sought and opened for the immense supply required of this material, in the whole exceeding 3,000,000 cubic feet – about 240,000 tons.

On the 24th of May 1854 the coffer dam for pier No. 1 was floated into its place so that from this day date the first operations in the river. On July 5 the dam for pier no. 2 was towed into its place, and on the 22nd of the same month the first stone of no. 1 was set. The masonry of the north or Montreal abutment was commenced on September 4, and on the 26th that of no. 2 pier. Pier no. 1 was completed on the 27th of October. On Friday, December 1, the winter's inclemency came suddenly upon the country, and stopped all out-of-door operations; and on the 5th the ice had so increased in the river that all communication was cut off, and steam boats had ceased to run. The result of this rapid change in the state of the weather was that the dams of pier no. 1, which it had been intended to tow into dock, got fixed in the ice, and the contractors were obliged to abandon them to their fate. On the 4th of January, 1855, the usual 'January thaw' as it is termed, occurred, and the water in the river rose fifteen feet, and dislodged and broke up the ice, which continued for some hours to come down with the current in large quantities. At midday it assumed so formidable a character in the vicinity of the bridge works that the dams and other temporary erections could no longer resist its force. Suddenly the whole gave way, and in less time than we take to write it there were not two sticks left together. The piers, thus suddenly stripped of their coverings, were now to be seen in their proper proportions for all appearance untouched and unimpaired, which the result of closer examination proved to be the case.[7]

The final phases of construction were equally energetic in the work to link the two sections of the Grand Trunk Railway.

Early in April and May the energies of all concerned in the work must be exerted to complete the bridge by October 1859.

In addition to the progress made with the masonry, the erection of the tubes has been carried on in due proportion, and the present condition of this important part of the work may be thus summed up. Four tubes were completed at each end of the bridge at Midsummer last, and two more were completed during the autumn, while two others during the winter were prepared for erection, as also that for the centre span, which is 330 feet long. During last summer the progress of the works was at its maximum. Upon the river, and between the dams and piers, the constant movement of steam-boats with barges in tow, laden with stone or other material, of which one thousand tons have been daily used, was not the least striking feature in the progress of the work. In this fleet alone – consisting of six steam boats and seventy-two barges, besides several small craft constantly plying upon the river – there were about 450 men employed; the tonnage of the flotilla in the aggregate amounting to 11,600, and the steam power employed to that of 445 horses. The artisans and labourers engaged upon the works of the bridge number 1850, and in the two stone quarries there are 500 men employed, number altogether 2800, including others variously distributed in the vicinity of Montreal, whose daily wages exceed one thousand pounds sterling. To this list should be added 142 horses, and four locomotives, engaged in conveying stone by the railway from Point Clair quarries, about sixteen miles distant.

This enumeration of forces now or lately employed in carrying on the works of the Victoria Bridge – independent of the large number at work at Birkenhead, in this country, in the preparation of the tubes, has never been equalled by any work of our day. The order and noiseless regularity with which the whole proceeds are the admiration of all who witness them. The daily growth of the bridge under the influence of such powerful forces is even remarkable to the engineers and others who have the opportunity of constantly observing its steady progress; and, considering the short season in which they can operate – seldom exceeding six months – it is rendered even more remarkable.[8]

While the British contractors undoubtedly built a solid railway between upper and lower Canada, they did no more work in North America as they were undercut by native and immigrant talent that built fast, rough and more cheaply. Sir William Van Horne and Andrew Onderdonk were both United States born, of Dutch extraction, who built the Canadian Pacific with Yankee hustle. Sir William's tracklaying feats on the Canadian Prairies in the early 1880s equalled the total mileage opened in Britain at that period. True, tracklaying there largely consisted of bolting together pre-assembled track on the bare earth, with crude trestles used for crossing gulleys and unavoidable rivers, but it was all done in record time. Onderdonk's methods speeded up ballasting enormously, and his Chinese labourers took the CPR through the Fraser River chasms at a spanking pace. The other outstanding Canadian contractor was Sir Casimir Gzowski, a Russian refugee of Polish extraction who continued the Grand Trunk Railway westwards to the United States border at Sarnia from the Brassey terminal at Toronto. The spectacular International Bridge at Niagara Falls was also constructed by Gzowski.

Peto, Brassey and Betts learned much from the Grand Trunk Railway contract, although they lost money on it. They also set up the Canada Works in Birkenhead to make rolling stock and metal parts for the GTR contract. The works was also used to supply their other contracts world-wide. Liverpool across the Mersey was the main port for the Americas and indeed most of the non-European world. In the seven years of construction in Canada, some 539 miles of line were constructed, including the magnificent Victoria Bridge across the St Lawrence at Montreal, but there was no follow-on in Canada or in the USA. Colonial experience, dearly bought, was applied in Australia, India, South America and the tiny Indian Ocean island of Mauritius.

The type of concession that attracted British and later American contractors to build railways overseas is typified by the prospectus for the Central Argentine Railway in 1864. It was a limited company, which made the risks more acceptable to outside investors. The Argentine Government guaranteed to pay 7 per cent on the capital for forty years, more than double the figure that could be obtained at home. The grant of land adjoining the railway ran to 900,000 acres, about the size of Suffolk. The board of directors who sought the subscription of £1,600,000 included the engineer W. B. Buddicom, contractor and himself a pioneer in French locomotive building, Sir Joseph Paxton, MP, director of the Midland Railway and designer of the Crystal Palace, and Samuel Waterhouse, MP, a director of the

Great Northern Railway. They were joined by bankers and merchants with South American interests. The contractors who were engaged to construct the line were Thomas Brassey, George Wythes and the American William Wheelwright, who was also concessionaire for the scheme to the Argentine Government. The contractors bound themselves to pay 7 per cent interest on deposits and calls, a powerful incentive to get the work done as quickly as possible. The building costs for the line across the Pampas from Rosario to Cordoba were about £6,500 per mile and the company also undertook to provide rolling stock, stations, management and to 'people the line', by encouraging migration. The contractors agreed to 'unite with shareholders in developing their resources'. With a comparable package deal from experienced railway contractors and operators, lines were built rapidly in most corners of the developing world, before exploitation became a dirty word.

Apart from the Brassey partnership ventures, Peto & Betts also constructed lines of their own overseas and at home. In Argentina, the line from Buenos Aires to Rosario sported a station at Rosario almost identical in appearance to the old Thorpe Station in Norwich, an early railway job of Peto. A major Russian contract for a railway from Dunaberg (Daugavpils today) to Vitebsk added 220 miles to his overseas tally, while the contract for the Algiers to Blida line was the first major African contract. Joint endeavours with Brassey in Australia started the three main lines of the New South Wales Government Railways beyond their pioneering line from Sydney to Parramatta. Some 54 miles of the three routes were added from 1859 onwards, while in Queensland from 1863 they built the first main line across the Great Dividing Range in that state from Ipswich to Toowoomba which was also distinctive in being a narrow gauge line. Prefabricated buildings and structures predominated on the new line, which was built as cheaply as the country would allow. Gradients as steep as 1 in 54, curves as tight as 10 chains and a summit tunnel through the Little Liverpool Range, inevitably named the Victoria Tunnel, made this a very different line from anything attempted in England. There were no previous railways in Queensland, so Sir Charles Fox, the civil engineer and contractor, was appointed to recruit staff and buy locomotives and rolling stock to be shipped out to the colony. Nearly 800 men were used at any one time on the contract, mostly locally recruited. The engineer to the line, Abram Fitzgibbon, had quarrels with the contractors who appear to have done some of the work wrongly and were also slow to complete, but three years for a pioneer contract several months' sailing time from the supply base was not at all bad. The problem for the English firm was that the Australians picked up the essentials of contracting very quickly indeed, so that the second Australian contract was also the last. The colonial toddler could now walk.

At home, Peto became deeply involved with construction in the Midlands. His contract for the Oxford & Birmingham Railway seems to have been fairly straightforward, but the same cannot be said for the Oxford, Worcester & Wolverhampton Railway (Old Worse & Worse to its opponents), the contract for which he took over from the dismissed contractor, Marchant, at Brunel's behest in July 1851. Marchant refused to go, so Peto summoned his navvies from the OWWR and from the Birmingham line which he was constructing, some 2,000 in all, who assembled at key points to take over the sites. Accounts vary as to how much fighting and damage there was, but Marchant backed down faced with such a force, and it was left to Robert Stephenson and Cubitt to adjudicate on the rights and wrongs of the matter. The finances of the company needed help from the contractor, the GWR was obstructive at Oxford over the gauge question, to which Peto replied by projecting an independent line to London from Oxford via Thame, High Wycombe, Uxbridge and Brentford, where it was to have joined the LSWR. He and the other contractors for the line, Treadwell Brothers, paid a parliamentary deposit and expenses to show how serious their proposals were, but in the end they were able to reach a compromise. Peto became chairman of the Severn Valley Railway, which Peto, Brassey and Betts constructed, giving the OWWR access to Shrewsbury, thus strengthening its strategic position between the GWR and the LNWR, a tasty morsel for either of the titans, which eventually went to the GWR. Railway politics of this kind played a large part in the construction of additional lines and of increasing their value when contractors sold out their shares on completion.

Other facets of business that the great contractors developed in the 1850s were the leasing of lines which they ran, sometimes with their own locomotives and rolling stock, and the development of land on railway routes that they had developed. The Shrewsbury & Hereford Railway was built by Brassey and Henry Robertson between 1851 and 1854. When completed, Brassey offered to work the line at his own risk and for eight years paid the proprietors 4 per cent plus half the surplus profits, which increased to the extent that in 1860 there was a 6 per cent dividend for the ordinary shareholders. Things did not run so smoothly on the adjacent Newport, Abergavenny & Hereford Railway (NA&HR) where Brassey provided locomotive power until 1855, when he withdrew his engines after a disagreement, leaving the company in a very difficult position. The problem was compounded by the LNWR withdrawing the rolling stock that they had loaned the NA&HR.

A somewhat happier situation existed on the London, Tilbury & Southend Railway, built by Peto, Brassey & Betts and then leased by them for twenty-one years. The line from Forest Gate to Tilbury and then on to Southend was opened first to Tilbury on 13 April 1854 and then in stages to Southend on 1 March 1856. It was promoted by the Eastern Counties Railway and the London & Blackwall Railway, but on opening to Tilbury was almost immediately leased by Peto, Brassey & Betts on a guarantee of 6 per cent interest per year and half the surplus profits. The latter never materialised, but the 6 per cent was paid for the twenty-one years of the lease. The object of the line was to capture a goodly share of the busiest pleasure traffic in the kingdom, down the Thames. At Tilbury a ferry took passengers across to the gardens at Rosherville and Gravesend where the mid-Victorian middle classes disported themselves, while the Southend extension gave much faster access to a growing day resort than did the river steamers. The contractors bought land there to develop the resort and also along the route to the east of the built-up area of London, hoping to develop suburban traffic. They were too early in both respects and the line proved something of a disappointment to them. By 1863 they had tired of their involvement in the LTSR and tried to lease it to the new Great Eastern Railway, which was gathering in almost all the lines in East Anglia under its umbrella organisation, but the attempt failed, one reason being that the railway offered only 4½ per cent on the shares as against 6 per cent from the contractors. By that time they were said to be losing £24,000 a year on the line after paying out the 6 per cent, which was a high rate in a period when government bonds yielded 2½ per cent. They continued their lease, but put as little money into the concern as possible, leaving the Tilbury to Southend section single tracked and with an inadequate train service. The General Manager, Mr Arthur Stride, 'found in 1875 no rolling stock of any description, no telegraph system, no block signals or anything of that kind'.[9]

The start of the Crimean War in 1854 found the government unprepared in almost every respect after four decades of peace. The contractors, particularly Peto, Brassey & Betts came to the rescue, looking on their military railway construction as a public duty, only charging the government the cost of materials, transport and labour. Peto, in talking to Thomas Brassey, son of the great contractor, said:

> The organisation of the detail and transport – a most laborious duty – was undertaken by my late lamented brother-in-law and partner, Mr. Betts, the general direction and administration resting with myself.
>
> We saw your father [Brassey] daily at this time [1854–early 1855]. He advised on all the points, and helped by every means in his power, and I should not do his and Mr Betts' memory justice, if I did not state that to them fully as much, as if not more than to myself, is the credit of the execution of the work really due. Our exertions were seconded by every railway company – the directors opening their stores for our free use at cost price.
>
> We succeeded in sending out 23 large steamers with men, horses, railway engines, commissariat and other stores, in a very short space of time, and within the first twelve days of the arrival of the first convoy we laid seven miles of line; and the soldiers handling shot and shell to each other were superseded to that extent in that time; and before the completion of the siege 39¼ miles of line were laid to every part of the front, and seventeen locomotives engaged in conveyance of stores, etc. etc. I received a letter from Field-Marshal Burgoyne, then General Burgoyne, on his return from the command of the Engineering Staff, stating it was impossible to overrate the services

rendered by the railway, or its effect in shortening the time of the siege and alleviating the fatigues and sufferings of the troops.[10]

At home, the recruitment of navvies to build the railway and the arrangements made for remittance of their pay to their dependants were carefully completed, while the use of prefabricated buildings helped greatly in taking the edge off the Russian winter. The military had proved itself incompetent; the contractors became the heroes of the hour.

Thomas Brassey carried on a considerable correspondence in his own hand from wherever he happened to be. In it he reveals himself always on the look-out for new opportunities, always talking to others who could help his business or whose business he could help. He seemed to know everybody in railway, financial and engineering circles. Some of his correspondence with Richard Moon of the LNWR gives the flavour of the man and his methods:

Westminster 4 May 1863

My Dear Sir,

I have this morning received the enclosed from Mr Field (an agent of Brassey's) respecting 8000 sleepers which he has on the Hereford line. Will you please tell me if you will accept them if their quality and price are approved. They are *not* creosoted which is the only reason why we could not make you a direct proposal in answer to your advertizement [sic].

Yours etc. Thomas Brassey.

Hotel Meurice, Paris,
19 April 1869

My Dear Sir,

Before leaving London I had a conversation with Mr Bidder [engineer] and Mr Trevithick [locomotive engineer son of Richard Trevithick], upon the Paris coal trade and since arriving here have seen Mr Blount [the banker] who for many years past has imported English Coal to Paris and the result appears to be quite conclusive that a business is to be done from Thames Haven of at least 300,000 tons annually upon terms that will be remunerative but of course requiring a capital to start it.

The coal proprietors and the London & North Western are the most largely interested and I should be very glad if when you have leisure for the purpose you would appoint a meeting with Mr Bidder who will come up to Euston or meet you elsewhere and will give you his views on the subject.

The result is so important for the L&NW and the Tilbury [LTSR
which Brassey and Peto leased] so far as it goes that it is I believe
well worth the effort to carry it out.

I am on the way to Vienna and shall be absent for a month or five
weeks but I arranged with Mr Bidder that you would most likely
give him an appointment.

Yours etc. Thomas Brassey.

Despite the enormous work-load that the great contractors
shouldered for a quarter of a century, they had time for other
matters as well. Somerleyton Hall and village were the object of
Peto's concern from 1842 until he sold it in 1863. The original
hall was decaying, the church half derelict, but renovation of
these and construction of a model village made it into a
community that is still a tourist attraction. Development of the
nearby brickfields provided employment for over thirty men,
making White Suffolk bricks which were used to build York and
Liverpool Street stations, and were even exported to Belgium.
The Lucas brothers leased the works in 1849, providing them
with a base for their later fast-expanding activities and Peto
with a useful, if small, income of over £200 per year. Peto's other
interests included his membership of Parliament, which in the
middle of the nineteenth century was fortunately less demanding
in time than it is now, and also the Baptists, of which sect he was
for long regarded as a leading lay member and supporter of good
causes, including chapel building.

Brassey was more of a family man. He restricted his family to
but three sons, thus allowing his wife, Maria, to retain better
health and vitality than her contemporaries. She helped her
husband in a secretarial capacity, travelling to Europe with him
on business. He rented a grouse moor jointly with Locke, but
saw very little of it due to work pressures.

'Why don't you do as I do, Brassey?' Locke used to say. 'Look at me! I
come down here to Moffatt, and here I remain for six or seven weeks,
and I won't have anything to say to your railways. I ask you to come
and stay with me. You come on Monday, and you go away on
Wednesday, having tried very hard to get away on Tuesday night, and
having spent the whole of Tuesday morning in writing letters; and
you know very well that there is not one of them that required writing
at all.'[11]

Like Peto, he was also devoted to good causes, such as navvies' charities and missions but in a less ostentatious way.

Edward Ladd Betts, a Kentish man who stayed true to the county of his birth, despite constant absence supervising world-wide contracts, was made successively magistrate, deputy lieutenant, and in 1858 high sheriff of his native county. The events of 1866, detailed in Chapter 7, broke him, despite Brassey's help, and he died at Aswan on a trip to Egypt intended to restore his flagging health.

The quarter-century reign of the great contractors effectively ended with the events of 1866. By that time they were all of advancing years, and had not established a structure which would ensure continuity of their activities. Their financial management was particularly vulnerable. In the Brassey organisation the accounts were purely local, each agent on each contract was personally responsible for money received and sent reports to Brassey at intervals. Brassey himself 'kept no regular check upon it, but simply noted that so much money had been sent to such and such a work. Beyond that no-one knew anything of the account. He relied on the cashier to keep the accounts and he was supposed to audit them every month, and always to be in a position to give Mr Brassey information he required'.[12]

The system worked for Brassey as he was rarely in grave financial difficulties, but Peto and Betts were bankrupted when they had no true idea of their position. Brassey appears fortunate in having representatives who never appear to have deceived him financially. The associates of Peto and Betts in the early 1860s were less sound.

Although Brassey appears to have been well loved by his navvies, his earlier camps showed less evidence of solicitude for the men than those of Peto. There appears to have been little improvement in this respect by 1865 as the following incident shows:

DREADFUL ACCIDENT ON THE BURY AND SUDBURY
RAILWAY. THREE LIVES LOST

One of the most lamentable and disastrous railway accidents that ever occurred in this locality took place on Saturday evening at Melford, upon the yet incomplete Bury and Sudbury line. A large number of workmen are still employed upon the line by Messrs Brassey & Co. and for some days past the men have been engaged in conveying ballast from Clare to Sudbury for the purpose of ballasting the line. This ballast was conveyed in trucks drawn by an engine, and the habit was for the engine to draw a full truck to Sudbury, and propel a train of empty trucks back to Clare. The points at the Melford junction were set 'fair' for the traffic on the main line, and were not only right when the train passed down, but a gangsman named Brown examined them the last thing before he left, and saw that the block of wood, or 'key' with which it is usual to fasten points in one particular direction while a line is in course of construction was in its place. The lever and compensating balance would alone be sufficient to keep the points fixed as they would be required for the main-line traffic; but as an additional security lest anybody should touch the lever-handle and so disarrange the points, it is usual to place one or two blocks of wood between the 'switch' (or shifting) rail, and the 'stock' (or fixed) rail. The manner of placing these blocks appears to vary. If laid between the two rails longitudinally, as was done in the case in question, any one shaking the handle of the lever would cause the block to turn up on edge, and so render the points 'foul' which must be understood, to mean that they would not be in a proper state for trains to pass on either line; but the more secure plan is to place the block transversely and drive it in firmly with a hammer, which would render it impossible to move the lever-handle as long as the block remained in its place. That the block used on this occasion had turned up as we have endeavoured to describe, is certain, from the fact that it has upon it an indentation, caused by a bolthead against which it had been pressed; but the manner in which this came about is entirely unknown. When the train of empties was returning it was being propelled (i.e. that the trucks were before the engine) at a pace variously stated by different witnesses as from 10 to 20 miles an hour; and there were in the trucks about a score of labourers, who were returning from their work, as they were in the habit of doing by the last train. The driver had turned off steam at Rodbridge, intending to stop at Melford; and when nearing the points in question, the man who acts as guard, and who was in the foremost truck but one, noticed that the points were 'foul', whereupon he signalled to the driver to stop and the engine was instantly reversed, and the steam turned on, but the flange of the truck wheels appears to have mounted and ridden over the switch rail, by which means they got upon the siding, where some tipping waggons had been placed for the night. A collision of great violence ensued. Several of the men, on seeing their danger, jumped off and escaped, but those who were in the foremost trucks met with a very different fate. About half a dozen of the trucks mounted the tipping waggons and run over each other, upsetting and crushing the poor fellows that were in them; and probably all the 13 trucks of which the train was composed would have followed had not the tender got off the rails and partially embedded itself in the ballast, which brought the engine to a stand. One man was picked up dead, having been killed instantaneously; another was lying with a truck wheel across his body, which was partly embedded in the earth; when first seen he exhibited signs of life, but was evidently dying and expired in a few moments, after gasping twice, and before any effort could be made to release him. Jammed between the buffers of two up-ended trucks, and suspended several feet from the ground, was the body of another poor fellow, from which all signs of life had been crushed out. These three being ascertained to be dead, the men who had escaped, together with others who were attracted to the scene of the catastrophe, set themselves to work to release those who were yet living, nine of whom were more or less injured; but with one exception (a man who was suspended by his heels, and could not be released for more than an hour, and then only by cutting away portions of the trucks), none sustained any injury from which they are not likely to recover. An inquest was held on Monday on the bodies of the three men who were killed, when the following verdict was returned: 'That the three deceased men came to their death through the defective working of the down loop points, and the Jury strongly censure the conduct of the contractor's servants in not properly securing them.'

Suffolk Chronicle 21 July 1865

Despite such incidents and the financial problems which flowed from the methods used by the greatest constructional employers and users of materials in the land, it must be said that in general they acted for the best according to a fairly strict morality. They paid well, kept hundreds of other businesses profitable, expanded British horizons overseas in a quantum leap never seen before and were thoroughly responsible in their attitudes when the crisis came. They greatly improved the image of the contractor in the quarter of a century that they held sway, national figures with standards which successors would have to emulate.

Herapath's Railway Journal could say of contractors, admittedly at a time of national pride during the Crimean War when the army was putting up a poor show: 'Our great railway contractors will figure in history as having performed a conspicuous part in the destruction of the Russian enemy, as well as in construction of railways all over the world – both operations being most beneficial to the interests of society at large.'

5

Celtic Fringe

The main railway networks of both Wales and Ireland were started later than those of England and Scotland, but once commenced, they were rapidly built and completed before the disasters of 1866. In Ireland, they owed much to the dynamism of William Dargan who built, financed and guided the Irish railway system for three decades.

Another native-born son was largely responsible for the Welsh network beyond the north and south coastal lines. David Davies of Llandinam, partnered by Thomas Savin of Oswestry, gave his country a plenitude of lines which brought the remoter parts of Wales into contact with industrial England, and later went on to provide South Wales with its ultimate coal railway – the Barry Railway.

They both had similar problems in raising capital to build railways in areas where little local money was available and enticements to outside investors were few. Yet they both succeeded in establishing systems that until recently were the backbone of the local economies. No comparable figure emerged in Scotland. The nearest we have is Sir James Falshaw, a Brassey agent who built several lines in the north and later became a very important figure on the North British board and in the city of Edinburgh.

Few contractors have had the opportunity to do as much for their country as did William Dargan in the time of Ireland's greatest distress. Ireland in the period before 1850 was grossly underdeveloped, overpopulated in relation to its existing resources and was the scene of western Europe's last great peace-time famine. Yet it was in this unpromising period that William Dargan built most of Ireland's main-line railways, thereby offering a great deal of employment and also an easy means of emigrating via the ports and of earning the money to do so. But there was much more to Dargan than merely building railways. He was a trained surveyor, a financier, ran many transport enterprises, promoted industry and was an improving landowner.

Although Ireland contributed many of the navvies who built British railways and several British engineers worked on transport projects in Ireland, no great British contractor was willing to build Irish railways, given the problems of finance and distance, not to mention the continuous background of political and religious troubles. It was therefore fortunate that this remarkable home-grown contractor emerged to build not only railways but also roads, canals and docks for a period of over forty years.

William Dargan's background was remarkably similar to that of Thomas Brassey, but usually Dargan was several years ahead of his better known English contemporary. The Irishman was born in 1799, some six years before Brassey, both being sons of gentleman farmers; both had a 'fair English education', as Dargan's obituarist phrased it, and both were trained in surveying, doing their practical work under the guidance of the renowned road engineer, Thomas Telford. They both went on to construct a larger proportion of their homeland's railways than any other contractor. The greatest difference was that Dargan did not undertake large overseas contracts, concentrating his efforts on a wide range of Irish transport, industrial and agricultural projects, although he did partner McCormick on a contract for the Manchester & Leeds Railway and also another on the South Yorkshire Junction Railway, both during the second Railway Mania.

It was in road building that Dargan first began contracting work on his own account when he returned to Ireland after helping Telford with the construction of the Shrewsbury to Holyhead road in 1819–20. The first important Irish job at the age of twenty-two was the building of an improved road from Dublin to Howth, a natural continuation of the Holyhead road, since Howth was the main outport of Dublin, before Kingstown (Dun Laoghaire) largely replaced it in the following decade. Other contracts followed, establishing Dargan as a versatile and reliable contractor.

The success of railways in Britain encouraged promoters in Dublin to present a Bill for the Dublin & Kingstown Railway to serve the harbour and the rapidly growing seaside suburbs. It was fortunate that the Irish Board of Works was prepared, even anxious, to help this first railway which could not have been funded solely by local capital. Dargan's rapid and high quality construction of the line on which so many of the civil service, parliamentary and other important government personnel travelled regularly, as well as the rapid rise in fortune of this line to the point where it paid a 9½ per cent dividend, led to a committee on public works recommending the building of a national state-funded system, a policy which was rejected and replaced by piecemeal government loans to selected companies.

Meanwhile Dargan's expanded organisation was engaged on other work, this time in Ulster. The Ulster Canal, linking Lough Erne to Lough Neagh and thence via the Lagan Navigation to Belfast, was being laid out by Telford, Dargan's mentor. From 1834 onwards, the engineering work was completed by William Cubitt, with whom Dargan worked until completion of the canal in 1841. This work promised to increase the importance of Belfast, then but one of several larger ports on the seaboard between Dublin and Londonderry and trading with Britain. Belfast suffered from a very muddy estuary which was also sinuous, preventing larger vessels from reaching the town. Dargan obtained the contract to make a straight deep-water channel from Belfast Lough to the town quays, work on which he was engaged until 1846. The tidal flats on either side of the river were observed by Samuel Smiles on his 1840 visit to Belfast where he found 'a large number of labourers . . . with barrows, picks and spades, scooping out and wheeling up the slob and mud of the estuary, for the purpose of forming what is now known as Queen's Island'. This lengthy and important series of contracts laid the foundations of both Belfast's and Dargan's later fortunes. Belfast rapidly became the second city of Ireland and its prime industrial and port centre, while Dargan was established as the peerless Irish contractor, able to cope with several contracts simultaneously.

While working on the Belfast scheme and the Ulster Canal,

Dargan returned to railway contracting with Ireland's second line, the Ulster Railway, incorporated in 1836 and opened section by section, first to Lisburn in 1839, onward to Portadown in 1842, but not reaching Armagh until 1848 after a further injection of capital. The problems that were to dog the construction of Irish railways became all too evident in the building of this line. Although most of the capital was subscribed by the public, they were slow in paying calls for further capital, consequently slowing down payments to the contractor and delaying the opening to traffic. The other major railway contract before the famine of 1845–9 was for the Dublin & Drogheda Railway, under an Act obtained in 1836 but not completed until May 1844. This was the southern leg of the through line from Belfast to Dublin along the prosperous east coast, yet neither the Ulster Railway nor the Dublin & Drogheda Railway could raise sufficient capital from the public, British or Irish, while their returns on capital were poor, £25,145 in receipts for 1843–4 for the Ulster Railway and £19,626 for the first seven months of the Dublin & Drogheda Railway, 58 miles of track taking less together than the six miles of the Dublin & Kingstown Railway. The D&KR's income of £45,255 in 1844 indicated its great prosperity.

Such was the background to railways and Dargan's constructional interests before the famine, but he did much else. He was on good terms with the Board of Works, whose control of the purse strings was crucial in the letting of contracts. He started the Ulster Canal Carrying Company in 1842, one of the first to integrate the carrying of produce from farm to English port, taking less than five days on the voyage from Enniskillen to Liverpool via Newry. This idea was later developed by Peto and Brassey in connection with the Royal Danish Railways and the port of Lowestoft. Development and drainage of land adjacent to transport routes also became his forte, while a steamer on Lough Neagh added to his cash flow. With wide and widening interests in many parts of Ireland, Dargan had a railway saloon car constructed in 1844 for his personal use. This was later to become the directors' saloon on the Midland Great Western Railway. By this time, few contractors in the British Isles, let alone Ireland, could match William Dargan's range of expertise and access to funds for construction.

On the eve of the famine, Ireland was economically two nations. The Anglo-Irish ascendancy and a growing body of Irish Protestant and Catholic farmers, merchants and even a few manufacturers such as Guinness and Jacobs, controlled the country's trade. Since Ireland was an integral part of the United Kingdom, they could, and often did, invest their surplus funds elsewhere in the kingdom or abroad. The Railway Commission on Ireland in 1838 had drawn a rather dismal picture of the likely profitability of Irish railways, not contradicted by the modest results of two of the three pioneering lines. The other part of the Irish economy was the peasantry – largely Irish speaking, illiterate, poverty stricken and living very insecurely on small plots of land cultivating potatoes and grazing a pig or a goat. They were almost outside the money economy, selling little and therefore unable to buy goods or to pay for rail travel. Their number had been growing alarmingly since the beginning of the century to a figure of over 7m, dependent on a single disease-prone crop. The disease, potato blight, struck in 1845 and for several years thereafter.

Irish railway construction was only just beginning to get started again after seven years without a single successful promotion. In 1844 the first sections of the Great Southern & Western Railway had received Royal assent, the remainder to Cork in 1845 being but one of a veritable flood of lines, starting with the Londonderry & Coleraine Railway in the far north, down to the Cork & Bandon Railway in the south west of the country, some 645 miles in all being sanctioned. Government assistance to build the basic network had been assured by Sir Robert Peel, the Prime Minister in 1842; now the surveys had been done and plans were made for presentation to parliament.

There was only one contractor in Ireland able to contemplate work on this scale, William Dargan. The Railway Mania in Britain at the time enabled some of the shares in the new promotions to be sold on the other side of the Irish Sea, while government backing for most of the enterprises indicated their non-speculative nature. Dargan himself showed a willingness to be paid in shares, loan stock or debentures, since by the 1840s his credit with Dublin bankers was the soundest in the land. His obituarist in the *Gentleman's Magazine* summed up the secrets of his success thus: 'The amount of business he got through was something marvellous . . . his success consisted in the selection of agents on whose capacity and integrity he could rely, and in whom he took care not to weaken the sense of responsibility by interfering with the details of their business, while his own energies were reserved for comprehensive views and general operations.' This was also very much the Brassey philosophy and in both cases it worked wonderfully well.

The relative success in not only obtaining Acts but also selling shares on the high tide of the Railway Mania encouraged the launching of over a score of new companies or extensions to existing lines in 1846, destined to add 670 miles to the Irish system if all were built. Given the over-extended state of the money market and the lack of building capacity, this was already beyond the resources of Ireland. An appeal by the railways for a government loan of nearly £5m in late 1846 fell on deaf ears, while Lord George Bentinck's famine relief scheme for building a national network of railways involving three times as much, raised in parliament in the spring of 1847, stood little chance of success. He was a Norfolk MP who had taken the Irish cause to heart, seeing the employment of over 100,000 labourers as a means of creating employment, encouraging Irish industry and providing a countrywide rail network in the shortest possible time. Yet the real famine tragedy occurred in the west, little affected by new railway schemes. In the end the government was prepared to loan £620,000 to the railways being constructed, which on the estimate of the Chancellor of the Exchequer should have been sufficient to employ 15,000 men. At a time when half the Irish population was on relief of one sort or another this was little enough, but with William Dargan in charge, it was money well spent and the labour force 'were paid the highest wages with the greatest punctuality', allowing the jobs that they had formerly occupied to be taken by others less fortunate, while the money spent in the country localities during construction helped mitigate the effects of the famine. The work provided directly, plus the new railway jobs created and the other railway-connected work called for, probably provided subsistence for over 100,000 people if dependants are counted. Little of this would have been possible without a strong and reliable contractor.

Dargan's lines spread steadily and in some cases fitfully out of Dublin and Belfast. The first section of the Great Southern & Western was completed in 1846 to Dargan's home town of Carlow, part of the Cork section being opened beyond Kildare in the following year to Maryborough (Portlaoghise). Simultaneously the Midland Great Western line was opened initially to Enfield and then Kinnegad the same year. In the north, the two standard gauge lines out of Londonderry were started, but only the line to Strabane was opened in 1847, while out of Belfast the lines to Ballymena and Holywood made some of the best progress seen in Ireland. Faith in agents was essential with work going on throughout the north, centre and east of the country. In addition, since the lines were opened in sections, Dargan was expected to attend the jollifications each time a length was opened.

Some of the heaviest civil engineering in Ireland was made on the approaches to Cork where the Carboniferous rock which underlies most of the route from Dublin, gives way to slate and much more rugged topography. The steeply graded, curved Kilnap Viaduct and the tunnel to Glanmire Road were novelties in Irish construction, yet Dargan was able to claim a clean accident record in the construction and there was much praise for the quality of the workmanship. The only sour notes in the opening of this major line were the lateness of the train from Dublin for the Mallow opening and the botched invitation list at the 1849 opening to Blackpool, Cork.

Engineering reports made in Ireland in the middle of the nineteenth century give some idea of the problems that Dargan overcame. On the Dublin to Mullingar section of the Midland Great Western Railway he crossed 8 miles of bog up to 70ft deep. Main drains parallel with the line of route were constructed, together with cross drains. A 30ft wide course of heather sods were then laid along the line of route, with half-baulk timbers on top. On this framework the track was raised a foot a day and underpacked each time, gradually achieving a good formation. The first engine to cross the line made a hollow for itself as it progressed in a wallowing way. The motion was said to be like the 'rolling of a ship at sea' and aroused doubts in the mind of the Board of Trade Inspector Captain Wynne as to the safety of the line. Over the period of a year the track consolidated and the same methods were later used elsewhere in Ireland.

Other lines, apart from the Belfast & Ballymena, stuttered along a very erratic building programme, going ahead when money flowed in from government or private shareholders and then grinding to a halt for several years. Yet despite the reluctance of Irish shareholders to invest and the government to loan really adequate funds, the lines were built to a high standard and by 1850 the famine was over.

While continuing to build railways and also to run the services on the Dundalk & Enniskillen Railway and the Dublin & Belfast Junction Railway, as well as a horse bus joining the two to the Ulster Railway at Armagh, the unstoppable William Dargan switched some of his enormous energies to promoting the agriculture and industry of Ireland. His first publicity vehicle was the Cork Exhibition of 1852, the year following its huge predecessor at the Crystal Palace and also the opening of the railway into Penrose Quay Station. One of his interests at the time was sugar beet, which he grew on his estates, exhibiting plants and their processing at Cork. This was a prelude to the Great Exhibition of Dublin in the following year. One can judge his financial resources by his expenditure on the exhibitions and railways in the five years after 1848. He started by putting £30,000 in the hands of the exhibition committee and had advanced £100,000 by the time that the exhibition closed. On the railway front he took over £700,000 in shares and debentures in railway schemes promoted by himself or in an effort to restart work on halted construction; such was his standing with the banks.

The zenith of William Dargan's career probably came with the visit of Queen Victoria to the Great Exhibition, followed by a visit of the Royal party, including Prince Albert and the Duchess of Wellington, to Dargan's villa at Mount Annville, overlooking Dublin Bay. He was offered a baronetcy in the same year, but unlike his contemporary Peto, he declined. The citizens of Dublin rewarded him with a bronze statue erected in front of the Irish National Gallery in the same year.

The railway schemes continued into the late 1850s, by which time over 800 miles of line had been completed by Dargan, a quarter of all the railways ever built in Ireland. The proportion of those remaining in use today is nearer half, as the early lines were the key lines and so have remained. A railway interest that lasted until the end was a return to his railway roots, the system that later became the Dublin & South Eastern Railway, incorporating the Dublin & Kingstown Railway. He helped direct its expansionary fortunes in the 1850s and early 1860s, serving a term as chairman.

Having provided Ireland with its transport network very successfully, it is a pity to record Dargan's relative failure as an industrialist seeking to raise the level of Irish manufacturing. At sixty, worn out by incessant work and travel, he owned some less than prosperous mills in County Dublin and started to grow flax on a large scale in County Cork to provide for a linen industry. His selection of management appears now to have been faulty. The downhill slide in Dargan's affairs was expedited in 1866, first by collapse of the railway share market in May of that year which left him financially weakened; then a fall from a horse seriously injured him and left him unable to give work his personal attention. He felt unable to continue payment on his debts, although he was probably solvent, if only just. He became depressed and never made a recovery from his bodily injuries, dying in February 1867. His widow was ill-provided for, having to be awarded a civil list pension to mitigate her straitened circumstances in 1870. It was a sad end for one of Ireland's greatest benefactors, the railway contractor who stayed at home.

Eventually much more successful than Dargan, because he changed his investments when railway contracting became a dangerous occupation, was David Davies, who found the centre of his country even more bereft of railways in 1855 than Ireland had been a decade before.

The basic structures of Welsh main lines by the mid-1850s was that of the South Wales Railway in the south from Chepstow to

Haverfordwest, and in the north the Chester & Holyhead
Railway. They were linked from Chester to Newport by a series
of railways built by Thomas Brassey. The GWR had its main
interest in the SWR, and the LNWR became the owner of the
C&HR. Between the two there were no railways apart from
mineral lines on the two coalfields. There were no major centres
of population, no major resorts had developed and the farming
was based on sheep and cattle, which could be walked to the
nearest railhead coastwards or on the English borders. The
mountainous nature of the country threatened to make any route
across it either impossibly steep or built at so enormous a cost
that it could never be profitable. Yet there was an avalanche of
schemes in the 1850s and 1860s aimed at linking the South
Wales coalfield and/or the Pembrokeshire ports with the other
industrial areas of the country, many of which were eventually
built, to become some of the most unprofitable lines in the
country. Despite the problems, they started the greatest fortune
made by a Welsh contractor and eventually made the Cardigan
Bay resorts and Pembrokeshire into popular holiday areas.

A line from Shrewsbury to Aberystwyth was proposed by the
LNWR in 1852, opposed by a GWR scheme for a line from
Oswestry to Newtown. The mutually destructive trench warfare
of the two railways destroyed the chances of either, so that a local
squire's scheme for two small end-on railways to serve his
neighbourhood was the one that received parliamentary sanction
in 1855. Squire George Whalley had Acts for the Llanidloes &
Newtown Railway and the Oswestry, Welshpool & Newtown
Railway, which although opposed by the LNWR almost as a
reflex action, passed with little difficulty. The method of
building the former line was to be small and local, like its origins.
Thus the *Oswestry Advertiser* and other local journals carried an
invitation for:

All persons desirous of tendering for the construction of the first
portion of the Llanidloes & Newtown Railway are requested to meet
Mr R. Hopkins the Company's engineer, at the company's office,
Llanidloes, at 11 o'clock on Tuesday next, October 2nd, when the
plans, sections and specification may be inspected, and the line will
afterwards be pointed out.

Any contractor possessing a small quantity of materials may undertake the contract as the works are to be paid for in cash, by monthly instalments.

Tenders are to be delivered to the directors at seven o'clock on the evening of that day.

The directors do not bind themselves to accept the lowest or any tender if not satisfactory.

THOMAS HAYWARD, Secretary

The instant reaction required to the advertisement was just the sort of stimulus needed by a young local road and sawing contractor, David Davies of Llandinam, one of the intermediate points on the little, isolated railway. Making bridges on local roads and erecting the livestock markets at Oswestry over a period of nearly ten years had made him a competent contractor with a flawless knowledge of the locality, so that he was able to undercut his six rivals in the few hours that he had to prepare his estimate and still make a profit. For two years Davies built the line section by section, until the money ran out, but in the meantime he leased the section of line already built at a rent of 4 per cent of the outlay at that point.

Meanwhile, in the middle of 1857, David Davies took as a partner Thomas Savin, to tender for the Vale of Clwyd Railway from Rhyl to Denbigh in North Wales. Savin was an Oswestry draper. The 10 miles took a year and a week to build, largely because Davies drove himself mercilessly for six very full days of every week, resting only the sacrosanct sabbath, as his nonconformist Welsh conscience demanded. Davies was the senior partner in the first year of the partnership, but when the time came to extend the line southwards from Denbigh to Corwen in 1860, Savin was sufficiently experienced in his changed role to undertake the contract alone. The line took four and a half years to complete, in contrast to the speed of Davies, but by then the firm was engaged on much larger jobs elsewhere. By 1859 David Davies had sufficient grasp of the trickier finances of railway contracting to be able to offer Squire Whalley completion of the Llanidloes & Newtown Railway in exchange for all remaining debentures and ordinary shares in the company. Their face value was some quarter higher than the cash price would have been, but discounts on stocks and shares were normal when cash was unobtainable. Bankers would then advance cash to pay for labour and materials while holding the shares as collateral. The line was completed and the lease renegotiated to include Savin as well. The L&NR was strategically placed on the route from Shrewsbury to Cardigan Bay and also on any north–south route through mid-Wales, so becoming the core of Savin's impetuous plans for extension.

The link from the L&NR to Oswestry was beset with greater problems. Much of the capital was dissipated on expenses and none was ready for use when Davies & Savin took over the works in October 1859. They were prepared to complete the line for the preference shares and debentures not issued at that point and all receipts up to the end of 1860. With such a scheme, it was essential that they work as fast as possible. By 14 August 1860 they had opened the line from Oswestry to Welshpool, but the need to make a deviation near Abermule resulted in delayed opening of the complete line until early August 1861.

The extension of the line westwards from Caersws (near the later Moat Lane Junction) to Aberystwyth officially started with the traditional cutting of the first sod at Machynlleth late in 1858. Thereafter the first signs of a split between Davies and Savin developed over the way in which the lines should develop. Savin anticipated Golden Rail by over a century in proposing to develop package holidays along the coast of Cardigan Bay at Aberdovey, Borth and Aberystwyth, where he built hotels, in which accommodation could be combined with through railway tickets. The cautious David Davies preferred the existing slower rate of development, consolidating his capital before embarking on another smallish contract, which would not be totally ruinous if it went wrong. The arrangement that eventuated was for Davies to build the line from Caersws to Machynlleth, while Savin went ahead with a grand coastal line from Aberystwyth to Portmadoc (Porthmadog) and the chain of luxury hotels that were to bring in the long-distance traffic. It is ironic that the Aberystwyth hotel later became the University College of Wales, strongly supported by donations from David Davies. The £80,000 that Savin had spent on the edifice of the Castle Hotel fetched a mere £10,000 in its new role.

David Davies continued to build steadily and economically, completing the line into Machynlleth on May Day 1862. The cost at £9,000 per mile was low when the country through which it was hewn is considered, including Talerddig cutting through solid rock, a monstrous undertaking for the period. Formal opening and running of regular trains had to wait until the New Year, but Davies was always one for the spectacular gesture.

There were only two further lines built by Davies as a contractor, although he did accompany the engineer Benjamin Piercy to Sardinia as a consultant in 1862, a contract on which Smith, Knight & Co later foundered. The Pembroke & Tenby Railway had been let in 1855 to George Wythes and the Treadwell brothers, but they had backed out leaving the field clear for local promotion in 1859. Only £5,000 of the capital was locally subscribed, leaving Davies and his partner, Ezra Roberts, to find the rest, a challenge which he no longer found difficult. The line was continued from Tenby to Narberth, where it joined the South Wales Railway, in 1866. All the capital for the extension was provided by Davies and Roberts. The other line was the Manchester & Milford Railway, which despite its pretentious name ran only from Pencader to Aberystwyth, although originally intended to join the L&NR at Llanidloes, where access to Manchester could be obtained via Oswestry. The section of the line across the Plynlimon Mountains was abandoned, but the line to Aberystwyth was started by Davies in partnership with the original contractor's son, Frederick Beeston Junior, in 1865, completing the line through all the financial hazards of 1866 with his own funds and the outright backing of the North & South Wales Bank. He had anticipated the coming crash and acted cautiously while starting to invest money in coal mining, the rising investment of the 1860s.

Thomas Savin, on the other hand, had learned the lesson of how to finance railways on promises all too well. While Davies built only 144 miles over a decade, Savin built 161 miles, including those jointly constructed with Davies, but his efforts were concentrated into less than eight years. The great coastal line from Aberystwyth to Pwllheli was speculatively based on the growth of the holiday industry in resorts over 100 miles from the nearest large industrial areas. His other major project, the Brecon & Merthyr Railway, aimed to haul coal across a mountain range and at Brecon deliver it to the Hereford, Hay & Brecon Railway or the Mid Wales Railway for its journey towards Birmingham or Birkenhead. Although such traffic developed, light trains and single track prevented it ever becoming the artery that the lowland route from Newport to Shrewsbury became.

One scheme which Savin agreed to start was the ill-fated Bishop's Castle Railway in 1861. He was paid £14,500 in ordinary shares, £500 in cash to defray parliamentary and engineering expenses and received a further £5,000 in March 1862 but made no physical progress whatever. The shares were almost valueless and he had other more spectacular plans in hand, so he obtained release from the contract in October 1863. The line was built by Benjamin Piercy for a lump sum of £250,000, but he ceased trading in February 1866, the line still unfinished.

Thomas Savin embarked on schemes without the necessary caution. He carried boards of directors with him, borrowed money almost recklessly and so over-extended himself that he went bankrupt in February 1866, some four months before the crisis developed in earnest, as the following report from the *Railway Times* shows:

> The Chief Justice of the Common Pleas, supported by his learned brethren on the bench has solemnly decided that the Lloyd's bonds issued by Mr Whalley and his colleagues are not binding on the company. The transactions are wholly vicious as well as illegal; and in so far as the shareholders are concerned, they remain uncontaminated by the odium which must attach to the affair. The National Discount, Overend Gurney & Co. and other money-lenders have been induced to make advances on securities that are entirely worthless; no less a sum than £60,000 has been raised under assumptions which fade before the law; but whether the individual participators in this affair may be brought to punishment for their misconduct, or whether they shall be silently permitted to retire from the condemnatory gaze of an excited public, are questions for the disappointed plaintiffs on the one hand, and the shareholders in the Mid-Wales (if there be any) on the other. Probably the contractor may deem it his best policy to discharge his creature-directors and to take the concern into his own exclusive keeping.

It was left to an amalgamation of the lines that he and Davies had built, the Cambrian Railways, to complete unfinished projects and to order the affairs of the little railways of Mid Wales. Picking up the pieces of Savin's profligate expenditure was David Davies, a working director of the new line, who, together with Sir James Falshaw, helped practically in the tidying up of the constructional and capital mess that they had inherited.

Unusually, Thomas Brassey and his man-on-the-spot for the Welsh borders, William Field, had less than usual to do with the early expansion of railways within Mid Wales. The Knighton Railway, from Craven Arms to Knighton, just inside Radnorshire, was their first contribution. It was, however, also the first section of the Central Wales Railway, the spearhead of the LNWR into the Swansea district. After a brief period of leasing by Brassey and Field, the Knighton Railway merged with the Central Wales Railway, authorised in 1859 to build a line from Knighton to Llandrindod Wells and an extension to Llandovery in the following year, where it joined the Vale of Towy Railway, already completed by the contractors Watson & Co who had built the Mid Wales Railway. The engineer was John Watson of the same company. The line was leased to the Llanelly Railway, which thereby provided a link to the coast of South Wales. By arrangement with Thomas Brassey and the Llanelly Railway, the through route from Shrewsbury to South Wales was taken over by the LNWR with portions of the line jointly owned by the GWR. Brassey family interests were represented by Thomas Brassey junior on the Vale of Towy Railway board until full amalgamation.

The other Brassey railway into Mid Wales was the series of small lines from Ruabon to Dolgelley that he and William Field successively built westwards, engineered as usual by Henry Robertson. The line started as a 6 mile branch from Ruabon to Llangollen under the title of the Vale of Llangollen Railway, opened to minerals on 1 December 1861. Before this was opened, in August 1860, an extension – the Llangollen & Corwen Railway – was sanctioned; this was not opened until 1 May 1865. The last two sections, known as the Corwen & Bala Railway and the Bala & Dolgelly [sic] Railway, were sanctioned on the same day, 30 June 1862, under different boards of directors and with different engineers. Henry Robertson acted for the C&BR, while Edward Wilson of the Great Eastern Railway acted for the B&DR. They eventually agreed on a joint station at Bala and through running of trains from the Great Western at Ruabon to Dolgelley and thence on to the Cambrian system for the opening on 4 August 1868. The Cambrian Railways had extended a branch up to Dolgelley from the coast line. The route was shorter than that of the Cambrian Railways' original line and had a useful connection to the north coast line via Corwen and Denbigh, but it was essentially a duplicate of the existing line to the coast and had to feed traffic on to the Cambrian, which preferred to use its own line where possible. This group of lines did, however, pay dividends, albeit low ones of 1½ and 2½ per cent before absorption by the GWR.

The vast majority of mileage between the Chester & Holyhead Railway in the north and the South Wales coalfield was constructed in a brief decade, and development in the area largely ceased thereafter. Three groups of contractors did most of the work, relying on financing by borrowing. It was fortunate for the district that most of the lines had been completed before the crisis of 1866, because there was precious little enthusiasm to do more than complete well-advanced lines after that traumatic shake out of dubious schemes and unsound contractors.

The LNWR and the Cambrian amalgamations brought some order to the affairs of the little railways that they took over, but two other lines were less fortunate. The Mid Wales Railway from Llanidloes to Brecon was constructed by John Watson in partnership with James Overend after a false start when Davies & Savin would not take the contract and Alexander Gordon failed to build the line. As a link from north to south, it was the least promising of all the schemes. It failed to construct a link to the Manchester & Milford Railway, thus precluding traffic from the south west, while its approaches to the South Wales coalfield were either over the mountainous Neath & Brecon line or the even more formidable Brecon & Merthyr line. The lease on the line by Watson Overend ended with the failure of the former in the wake of Savin's bankruptcy. The line continued an independent existence until the Cambrian Railways took over in 1888.

The Neath & Brecon Railway was another to suffer from the wave of bankruptcies in 1866–7. The contractor to the line was John Dickson, who had built the line northwards from Neath up the Dulais Valley and was constructing a line across the moors from Sennybridge to Llangamarch on the Central Wales Railway, when he failed in 1867. Earthworks are still visible from that debacle which promised a fourth line from South Wales to Mid Wales, single track, steeply graded and poorly built like the others. Of the contractors who took part in the ten years of overbuilding up to 1866, only David Davies came out of the collapse unscathed, mainly because he did not exceed his limits, building only the more sensible and profitable sections of line, while realising his gains before investing in further sections of line. Others were financed at high interest rates by men of dubious financial probity, making lines that were built almost simultaneously between the same general areas and for the same purposes. Not even the phenomenal growth of South Wales in the 1860s could provide enough traffic for so many railways all at once. The lack of regulation in planning railways and the speculative financing of them was so concentrated in this one area that it served as a warning to others later. Very little further construction was undertaken, while most of the lines constructed became victims of closure early on in the Beeching era. Only the Aberystwyth and Pwllheli lines, together with the Central Wales line survive, supported by massive subsidies.

Of the contractors active in Mid Wales, David Davies was undoubtedly the most authentic local product. He could wield a spade or pickaxe with the best of his navvies, would wrestle with the men, chase game or just sit down for a chat over tea, bread and cheese. He recruited his gangers from his native village of Llandinam, seeing that they were well placed in railway jobs or came on to his next contract. His ability to talk to the men in their own language and give them a share of his triumphs led to their supporting him when times were bad. His decision to leave railway contracting came in part at least from fear of a financial collapse if speculative building of Savin's kind continued. Having provided what he considered part of the necessary railway framework, he sought other channels for his business vitality, returning to railway promotion in the 1880s when he considered that the monopolistic Taff Vale Railway was giving inadequate service to the burgeoning collieries of the Rhondda Valley.

6

Nemesis

The tendency of railway management and contractors to build beyond likely demand was seen in several ways in the early 1860s. In Mid Wales there was a clear need for some railways to serve farmers, a scatter of mines and quarries and to link the coast to the main railway network. Instead there was open competition by the main-line railways to secure territory and to invade every conceivable through route as well as several unlikely ones. The railways produced were poor, single line affairs, financially unsound if without the backing of a major company and largely incapable of providing either really fast services or facilities for heavy traffic. Goods trains limited to a mere thirteen wagons on the Neath & Brecon Railway, or the all-stations services that were the best that the Midland Railway could provide from Swansea to Hereford were no match for the longer but better built routes of the 1840s. It was a case of much capital being too thinly spread on too many projects, while some of it was completely wasted.

The railway deficiencies of other areas likewise came under the microscope of promoters and contractors in their efforts to discover new lines to build. Duplicate routes between places already served, urban railways and goods yards, railways connected with new docks and overseas railways were all promoted. The problem was that the pace of railway construction was well ahead of economic growth in several areas; thus new facilities had to attract traffic from existing means of transport until growth caught up with railway expansion. If the railways cost a great deal to build using expensively borrowed money, then their likelihood of success was slight, and the probability of losses or complete failure greatly increased.

The Victorian economy was less controlled by government than it had been before the railways or after the imposition of controls in the wake of financial scandals. Boom and slump had followed each other in an almost predictable pattern since the first Railway Mania. Crises in 1836, 1847 and 1857 had been followed by a collapse in railway investment and resulted in a difficult period for the contractors. Each time the survivors had come back to a new crop of projects, with ever more ingenious ways of financing them. A Stock Exchange boom in the mid-1840s had made it possible to pay contractors by requesting the owners of shares to pay their calls. In the main building period of the 1850s, the willingness of contractors to take shares and raise loans on them while building the line, then selling them to recover their expenses had become the normal way of financing railway construction. The construction boom that commenced around 1863 was fuelled by the emergence of the finance company.

There was a variety of other ways in which contractors could finance the building of railways without sufficient or even any capital having been subscribed by the investing public. The contractor would take shares at a discount, thus inflating the capital of the railway company. Another method was to get the engineer to certify a higher price for earthworks and structures than was really the case so that all the multifarious expenses of surveying, legal and parliamentary expenses as well as land could be included in the construction cost, the original costs of setting up the line having been paid by the contractor, probably on borrowed money. Payment by contractors on stocks and shares issued before the opening of a line was also a common feature. For example Fox, Henderson & Co paid 4 per cent on the shares of the railway in the early stages of the construction of the LCDR. The yield would then encourage other investors to buy the shares, thus helping the contractor to realise some of the paper payments made to him. When this battery of fund-raising ploys had been exhausted, there still remained Lloyd's bonds. The railway affixed its seal to the bond, stating that the company owed the contractor a sum of money which, together with interest, would be paid at some future date. This bond could then be used to raise a loan, the bond being either taken at a discount or a high rate of interest levied by the bank or loan company. The railway boom of the early 1860s was floating on a sea of paper, much of it of dubious worth.

Sound schemes for reputable railways, such as the London extension of the Midland Railway, could be paid for in cash or the first class shares of the company concerned. The contractors signed up for such a project included Thomas Brassey and his partner Stephen Ballard, as well as Joseph Firbank, least speculative of any contractors, whose main works were completed after 1866. Smaller railways, less sound contractors, or those who had exceeded their credit with normal banking institutions, had to have recourse to the more risky methods of financing. To aid such companies and contractors, a group of impressive-sounding companies came to the rescue. The International Financial Society, the Joint Stock Discount Company, Imperial Mercantile Credit and the London Financial Association, as well as a number of older banks including Barned & Co of Liverpool and Overend, Gurney of London, started to finance railways, contractors and other companies in much the same way as finance companies. The finance companies and banks advanced money at high rates for the period on security of shares, debentures and Lloyd's bonds to contractors, manufacturers and landowners. They also issued shares and stock to the public where possible. Directors of finance companies included Sir Samuel Morton Peto and William Dargan, indicating a circular course for some of the money and a lack of the checks on lending so necessary for financial stability. Both the gentlemen named were railway directors, major contractors, manufacturers and directors of finance companies. It was to say the least, an unhealthy situation.

The financial companies advertised in the railway and City press for money, offering rates of interest and promises reminiscent of the secondary banking and property boom of the early 1970s, which assumed that prices and construction would continue ever upwards. The consequences were similar. Increasingly nervous traditional bankers and cautious investors on one side, the overblown speculators and their unstable financiers on the other. Two typical advertisements of 1865 tell their own tale:

THE RAILWAY CREDIT COMPANY

Capital £2m in 40,000 shares of £50 each (first issue 20,000 shares, of which it is expected that only £10 will be called up), has been formed to facilitate the purchase and construction of railway and other public works, to enable contractors to carry on suitable works, and to make advances on railway and other securities. The company will also act as financial agents generally.

THE CREDIT FONCIER ET MOBILIER OF ENGLAND (Ltd) are instructed to receive subscriptions for the A stock of the Metropolitan Extension Railways of the London, Chatham & Dover Company. The amount to be issued is £1,212,000. The following table, given in the prospectus, shows the form of this stock: Debentures £1,433,000; B stock 6% preference, £825,000; C stock 6% preference after B stock, £1,050,000.

A stock for future issue as fully paid up stock: Entitled to the remainder of profits to 6% – £2,425,000.

Arrangements made with Sir Morton Peto for a guaranteed dividend of 6%. A much larger dividend is anticipated from the wonderful augmentation of suburban traffic.

The LCDR ceased paying anybody anything on 2 July 1866.

The most ambitious series of contracts undertaken in the years immediately before 1866 was the construction of the London railway termini and their associated yards and goods facilities. Victoria, Cannon Street, Charing Cross, Holborn Viaduct, Blackfriars, Broad Street and St Pancras, together with the enormously expensive bridges, viaducts and tunnels leading to them, were authorised and built within the period from 1857 to 1866. The exception was Liverpool Street which was delayed by the insolvency of its owner, the Great Eastern Railway. The start of rail-borne suburban traffic into London and the difficulty of moving people about in horse-drawn London, had highlighted the need for stations closer to where people actually worked than, for example, London Bridge or Shoreditch. Connected with the proposed new stations was the pair of schemes for the first underground railways, the Metropolitan and the Metropolitan District railways. The cost of these lines at nearly £1m a mile was beyond the ability of the railway companies to raise by themselves, and particularly was it beyond the capacity of the struggling London, Chatham & Dover Railway which was to have its West End terminal at Victoria, its City termini at

Blackfriars and Holborn Viaduct, and access by the Widened Lines of the Metropolitan Railway to Moorgate as well. The funding of this railway in particular, requiring the issue of £4,100,000 in preference shares and debentures for the City undertaking alone, seemed to pour out in a never ending stream in the early 1860s. That was warning enough of impending trouble. The LCDR was the despair of its contractors. The local line from the Medway towns to Faversham sprouted extensions at both ends to make it a shorter route from London to Dover; the railway then started a grandiose drive for suburban traffic which forced its rival, the South Eastern Railway, to build its own West End and City termini at enormous cost. Sir Charles Fox, one of the original contractors, had interests in the Crystal Palace which he had built and which the LCDR served. Thomas Russell Crampton continued the construction of the line, finally aided by Messrs Peto & Betts. Like a cuckoo in the nest of another bird, the line continually cried out for further feeding, while sensible investors, noting the insatiable maw of the creature, invested little, and that at ever increasing discounts, thus worsening the situation. Not only the LCDR, but also the London, Brighton & South Coast Railway, the Great Eastern Railway, the North London Railway and even the mighty Midland Railway, weakened themselves dangerously when they built their London termini. The immediately available increase in traffic just did not justify the vast outpouring of capital that was required.

The contractors who built this array of stations and their approaches, together with the underground railways, were mostly those who had grown in the 1850s, but there were some new faces as well. Peto & Betts built the Victoria & Pimlico Railway into that terminal in partnership with John Kelk, an associate of theirs and of Brassey. Kelk is chiefly remembered for the construction of the South Kensington museums and the Albert Memorial. His main railway work included the Metropolitan Widened Lines, some of the Metropolitan District Railway and the Smithfield Goods Depot. His much wider range of contracting protected him from the worse effects of the 1866 crash, as did the investments of George Wythes in iron works and his contracts in waterworks. Wythes' main London contract was the construction of Cannon Street Station for the South Eastern Railway. He worked with Charles Lucas, a former Peto agent, who had contracts to build Charing Cross Station and hotel and partnered Kelk and Waring Brothers in constructing the Metropolitan District Railway. He was a major general builder of hotels and public buildings who only came to railway contracting on his own account in the early 1860s, but had sufficient reputation by 1865 to join Brassey and Wythes in constructing the East London Railway under the Thames. His main railway work was done for the Great Eastern Railway in the following decade, but he was sufficiently busy in 1865 to turn down an invitation to build the little Mellis & Eye Railway in Suffolk, a very easy contract, but too far from London.

Away from London some of the railway speculations verged on the incredible in their assumptions. The Somerset & Dorset Railway from Burnham-on-Sea to Poole crossed a narrow neck of the south-west peninsula, planning to capture traffic between South Wales and the Continent by running boat services from its termini. Waring Brothers, who built the system, had been in railway contracting since the 1830s, first under the father of John Waring and then Charles, the third son, became the most important partner. Much of his work was overseas, thereby gaining a knighthood in Belgium from the unpleasant King Leopold and the Order of St Maurice & St Lazarus from Italy, but reproaches from his activities in Portugal and Spain. The Institute of Civil Engineers frequently used the word 'integrity' in their obituaries of past members; they omitted it in the case of Charles Waring. His dubious activities in the Bournemouth area have been fully covered by Lawrence Popplewell. Suffice it to say that the Somerset & Dorset Railway cost vastly more to build than at first proposed, at least according to the contractor. It failed to live up to expectations because there were more comfortable ways for the people wishing to travel from Cardiff to Paris, and goods went direct by sea in any case. Only the later construction of the Bath line and the link with the Midland Railway saved the S&DR from atrophy.

The contractors for the first section of the Metropolitan

Railway, Messrs Smith, Knight & Co, were tempted into overseas contracts for the Royal Sardinian Railways in Italy, but the advent of war with Austria and their over-extended position in Mexico made them vulnerable before the major crisis of May 1866, resulting in their bankruptcy. Given the number of warnings that things were going very badly wrong in both home and overseas railway contracting, it is surprising to find such a long-established and generally upright contracting company as Peto & Betts plunging ever deeper into the speculative mire with the LCDR at home and the Atlantic & Great Western Railway in the USA, especially after their experiences with the Grand Trunk Railway in the 1850s.

The ending of the Civil War in the USA in 1865 heralded the greatest railway building boom that country had ever seen. The American financier McHenry was building a line which would run, hopefully, from New York to Chicago and St Louis, but he had had little success in selling the bonds to finance the line on the London market. Despite this, he brought in Peto as a partner to build the last part of the line, despite a cloud of financial distrust that overhung everything to do with the line. A promotional tour of the USA by Peto and other financiers in the autumn of 1865 yielded a book replete with every evidence that he was enthralled with the prospects, blind to the reality. The directors of the finance companies were not so sure of their own boundless future; they had taken care in 1865 to convert themselves into new-fangled limited liability companies, something that worthy contractors like Brassey and Peto refused to do, thus leaving themselves open to full responsibility for debts incurred.

The early months of 1866 showed many signs of an impending slump. Not only had several contractors gone bankrupt on the risky contracts in Wales and abroad, but the shares of the less stable railway companies lost ground continuously on the Stock Exchange. A letter to *The Economist* in January 1866 darkly referred to 'the manufacture of bubble companies' and 'about the railway traffic I find statements which are wholly imaginary'. But even those who saw what was coming and knew that it would cause them difficulties were largely locked into a situation that was similar to an express train without brakes rushing towards a broken bridge. If they baled out early, their chances of survival were probably no greater than sticking it out. The early wave of bankruptcies showed that quite clearly.

Nemesis struck on a day that became known in the annals of finance as 'Black Friday', 11 May 1866, when Overend, Gurney & Co Ltd failed to open for business, with known debts of £10m. Peto & Betts stopped paying the same day with debts of £4m, although it was thought at the time that they were worth £5m if only they could sell the securities that they had as collateral for the debt. But they could not, and with prices of those securities slumping while the bank rate climbed to a then incredible 10 per cent, they were unlikely to sell much in the near future.

The effect of the failure of old-established and respected names like Overend, Gurney and Peto & Betts was traumatic. 'Lombard Street has been thronged and almost stopped by curious wonderers in a way we never saw it before, and on the whole we doubt if there ever was a collapse of credit more diffused and more complete.' So wrote *The Economist* the day after the failure, when it could at last say what it had long suspected, that 'the plain truth is that Overend Gurney, unlimited for the sake of high interest, took bad securities, and in consequence someone must reap the due consequence of that badness'. The people who suffered were the incautious investors and contractors, the material suppliers left with bad debts or with stock certificates which were unsaleable, sound businesses that had dealt with the unsound and now had no recourse for recovering their debts and those caught in the middle of cautious expansion who suddenly had to pay double the interest rate. Even the Midland Railway had to ask its contractors to accept shares in lieu of cash during the worst of the crisis, but at least those contractors got their money back later. No one knew at first who was sound and who was unsound.

War in Denmark, Germany and Austria had upset several of the contractors, including Brassey, Peto & Betts. Frontier changes added to the uncertainty as to whether work already done would be paid for. The devotion of Brassey's agents in troubled time had much to do with his survival in the crisis of

1866. His representative in Austria, Victor Ofenheim, was constructing a railway between Cracow and Lemberg when he found that the warring armies of Prussia and Austria cut him off from the men he had to pay:

> However he was full of energy, and was determined to get on somehow or other. They said that there was no engine; that they had all been taken off; but he went and found an old engine in a shed. Next he wanted an engine driver, and he found one, but the man said he would not go, for he had a wife and children; but Mr Ofenheim said 'If you will come, I will give you so many hundred florins, and if you get killed I will provide for your wife and family'. They jumped on to the old engine and got up steam. They then started and went at a rate of forty or fifty miles an hour, and passing between the sentinels of the opposing armies; and Mr Ofenheim states that they were so surprised that they had no time to shoot him. His only fear was that there might be a rail up somewhere. But he got to Lemberg, and that was the saving point of the line – they made the 'pay' – otherwise the men would have gone away to their homes, and the line would have been left unfinished through the winter, and they would have had to wait until the next spring before they could have returned again, but that difficulty being overcome got the line duly opened.[1]

It also meant that the Austrian government continued payments to Brassey, allowing his cash flow to keep up work elsewhere on the score or more of projects then proceeding. Others had smaller reserves or were less lucky.

It was not known for some time just how badly Peto & Betts had failed. Five weeks after Black Friday *The Economist* wrote:

> It is pleasant to have to comment on a failure in comparison (with Overend Gurney) free from blame. We do not say that Sir Morton Peto has not committed great errors; no one stops payment unless he has done so. These errors were plainly two, he engaged in operations beyond the force even of his great capital, and in consequence borrowed at rates of interest so high as to be injurious to his credit as well as destructive of his profit. Still the immense mass of his business was very good, and some of it doubtless stupendously profitable. There was no lending of millions on securities worth only thousands. That the last few weeks must have been very painful to Sir Morton Peto we can well believe, but no one can doubt who really understands such manners that he will emerge from the cloud a very rich man still, and with a character for honour beyond the reach of any question. [See Appendix I].

For Peto, resignation from parliament in 1868 and a disastrous re-entry into contracting on the little Cornwall Minerals Railway in the mid-1870s, finished him entirely as a contractor and a public figure. He was honourable enough to sell his own and his wife's valuables to pay debts when costs escalated on that troublesome railway, but the Peto of old would not have allowed the situation to get so far out of hand in the first place. His erstwhile partner Brassey lost £1m during the crisis, but at least he could get minimal credit from his bankers and still died one of the richest men in the country in 1870. He also carried on joint contracts that Peto & Betts could no longer fulfil.

The domino effect of the failure pursued contractors and railways alike for over a year after the collapse. The Cambrian Railways were in trouble from their inception, but the aggressively expanding Great Eastern, the North British and London, Brighton & South Coast railways went into receivership along with the LCDR and many very much smaller lines. Other railways either reduced their dividends, or in the case of the LBSCR, GER, and NBR failed to pay them at all, thus reducing future capital raising possibilities. The three railways that went into receivership along with the LCDR all recovered from the crisis and resumed dividend payments in the 1870s. The evaporation of what *The Economist* described as 'the marvellous confidence in those skilful operations kept up while money could be had at any price (between 7% and 16%)' was probably no bad thing. The contractors were anxious to get as many contracts as possible and the landowners to sell their land: 'the public interests cannot be honestly promoted by clever financial operations where they are not wanted'. The sorting out of the contractors and the closing down of thoroughly bad schemes like the Neath & Brecon extension and the Mistley, Thorpe & Walton Railway at least divided sheep from goats in a rough and ready manner.

The larger railways which succumbed to the troubles of 1866 included the LBSCR, which by means of new construction had expanded to fend off competition on both flanks of the main line. A contemporary account in the *Diss Express* tells the full story:

Cut and cover operations with mechanical help from steam cranes at Blackfriars on the Metropolitan District Railway in 1866 (*London Transport Collection*)

Panic in the city as news is read of the closure of Overend, Gurney in 1866

A man-made mountain of chalk, excavated to prepare the site of Brighton
Works on the London, Brighton & South Coast Railway (*Lens of Sutton*)

Firbank's Regent's Canal bridges near Marylebone on the Great Central
Railway, 1897 (*from the collection of S.W.A. Newton and by permission of
Leicestershire Museums, Art Galleries and Records Service*)

The net income of the Brighton Company is, it will be seen, actually greater in these days of disaster than it was in the days of their prosperity, but the increase has been obtained by so prodigious an outlay that the result represents, not gain, but loss. In acquiring £113,000 of additional revenue the company has added upwards of £8,000,000 to its capital – that is to say, has raised and spent money to that enormous amount. The question is, then, how or where this expenditure has been incurred, and the answer can be plainly given. For two or three years after 1854 the management of affairs continued to be successful, but in 1858 we detect the first sign of mischief in a payment made out of capital for the relief of revenue and improvement of dividend. The sum is very small, only some £1,600; but the practice grew so rapidly that the appropriation became upwards of £12,000 in the very next year, and exceeded £175,000 in 1866. Altogether, in the course of nine years a sum of £435,000 has been paid to the proprietors in the form of dividends which, instead of coming legitimately out of revenue, was taken from capital. That leaves some £7,600,000 to be accounted for, and this account is put before us in expenditure upon new works. The company spent between 1855 and 1866 no less than £2,500,000 upon country branches, £2,000,000 more upon metropolitan and suburban lines, £500,000 upon the station at London-Bridge, and £1,800,000 upon new stations and incidental objects at the West-end.

The suburban lines will, it is thought, owing to the immeasurable growth of traffic at great centres of population, be profitable to the shareholders some day or other, the misfortune being that they were constructed at a time when the company could not afford the outlay, to the serious damage of the present generation of proprietors. But with regard to the country branches it appears difficult to conceive even these little lines, four only pay so much as their working expenses; on the other eight there is actually a loss of £12,000 a year. Upon the whole, the report concludes that these country extensions must be regarded as having involved the company in 'a dead loss of upwards of £3,000,000'.

This, in a few words, is the story of the transactions which have brought the Brighton Company from prosperity to distress, but we wish, before we conclude, to bring into prominent notice the following reflection made by the Committee of Investigation on the result of their labours: 'It is fair to observe that these lines were to some extent forced on the company by the fear of competition. It is easy to see now that by far the wiser policy would have been to stick to the original line, keep down capital, and let competing schemes do their worst. It is certain that in such cases nine out of ten of the competing projects would either have broken down altogether, or been offered to the company at a ruinous discount, when calls began to press, and long before the works were completed.'

Waring Brothers survived the crash, worthier men like Peto and Betts did not. Dargan was probably not bankrupt, but died thinking that he was. The crash of 1866 marked the end of an era, one which had brought the contractor to the peak of his importance nationally as well as in railway affairs. Although construction of railways continued in the 1870s and beyond, the contracting companies that came forward to take up the reins were less dominant in railway affairs, usually had a much greater spread of work in other parts of the economy and seem to have learned at least some of the lessons taught by the confidence-shattering events of 1866.

The Economist summed up a thoroughly disreputable period as one which was 'encouraging railway speculation in some of its crudest forms, and fastened speculative contractors and their marauding schemes with the idea that the great companies which were attacked would, in the end, be compelled to buy up the projects, which, like pestilential parasites, fastened upon them'. Undoubtedly the schemes of Brassey, Peto and Betts could be classified under their stricture.

7

Late Victorian Professionals

There was no true successor to Brassey or Peto. The age when British contractors had the world to themselves was rapidly ending by the 1860s, and the opportunities to construct major main lines at home were waning at an equal pace. Even so, the railway contractor was far from finished in the 1870s; indeed the scale on which he worked was often larger than in pioneering days as trains grew longer and heavier and the work attempted in crossing mountain ranges and bridging, or tunnelling under, major waterways became more daring. The departure of the early giants from the scene brought forward men of a rather different but no less interesting stamp. They also provide a bridge between the early giants and the modern civil engineering combines.

Contracting dynasties were rare. The Warings have already been noted. McAlpines are still happily with us and recently rebuilt Leicester Station. Of the Victorian contractors, the Firbanks – father, son and nephew – must rank as the premier family firm in achievement, since the Warings disappointed several of their employers; the Firbanks, as far as the author can trace, never did.

Joseph Firbank's early story sounds like the classic Victorian rags to riches saga. He was born in 1819, son of a poor Durham miner who sent him down the pits in 1826 at the tender age of seven to help the family budget. Endless hours of toil, six days a week, did not prevent him learning to read in his few spare hours, and when the opportunity to work on railway building around Bishop Auckland came in 1833, he seized the chance to work above ground, going on to become a sub-contractor at the Woodhead Tunnel where his mining knowledge came in useful. He further repaired some of his wide educational gaps in the early 1840s, demonstrating that capacity for working all his waking hours that stayed with him for life. He lived for little else.

Construction work for Firbank in his early years was hazardous indeed. He lost most of his capital in the financial crash at the end of the second Railway Mania while working on the LNWR line from Rugby to Luffenham under the Stephensons. On another occasion, while working for the Midland Railway, he was captured and held for twenty-four hours by an irate landowner for daring to do preliminary work and cross private land. Such incidents seem to have been all in the day's work in the 1840s. Other work in this period included sub-contracting on the York to Scarborough line, as well as the Leicester to Peterborough line where he had the Oakham section, again working under George Stephenson. He gained a reputation for honesty and for completing any work he started, which was not always common at that time. Yet he was hard-headed enough to treble an already profitable estimate when he saw the chance of increasing his capital. The other side to this attitude was that the railway companies rarely compensated the contractor when his expenses exceeded his estimate. He somehow found time to get married to a widow while working near Melton Mowbray in 1849. Their son, Joseph Thomas, was born in the following year to this strong-minded woman who further educated her rather rough husband and helped him move more easily into the upper social classes.

While working in the Midlands he found that his partner Rodwell was deficient in several respects, not least in a liking for the bottle, so thereafter he undertook all contracts either by himself or with the aid later of son and nephew. His first real opportunity to obtain a large contract was when the Monmouthshire Railway & Canal Company was converting its lines from tramroad to conventional railway. The company had suffered years of delay due to failing contractors and lack of finance at the right time. Firbank was recommended for the job by Charles Liddell, engineer to the company, who had worked with Firbank on the LNWR contract, where he had been struck by the young contractor's positive qualities. The work was to make deviations from the old tramroad route and alter the route of the canal at Newport. The directors were impressed with what they saw. The previous history of poor maintenance and broken tramplates which had dogged the line since the introduction of locomotives in 1829 was ended when they gave Firbank a seven-year maintenance contract. Their confidence was not abused, for Firbank's work was good and his contract was renewed again and again until amalgamation with the GWR, when he started to do more work for that august organisation. This maintenance contract provided a regular income and a good background to his larger and more remunerative contracts elsewhere. He also became associated with the Monmouthshire ironmaster and MR&C director Crawshey Bailey, who extended credit to him as a useful customer. Monmouthshire also provided him with a home base after his previous gypsy-like career. He took a fine neo-classical house, St Julian's near Newport, became a justice of the peace and eventually rose to be Deputy Lieutenant of Monmouthshire; this was truly a gutter to gentility progress in the best Smiles tradition.

An association with the LBSCR started in 1859 and lasted the rest of Firbank's life. The Shoreham, Steyning & Horsham Railway was built under R. Jacomb Hood, an engineer with whom he did much work. He later took contracts on many more of their extensions and improvements, gaining useful experience of urban railway engineering problems in 1863-5 when he and his nephew Ralph built the South London Railway. He later returned in the 1870s under Banister and Wolfe-Barry to fill in the network of lines in the Croydon–Tunbridge Wells–Lewes triangle.

Other work which became his bread and butter included the widening of lines for the LNWR in 1859-61 and building the first 12 miles out of Cambridge on the line to Bedford in 1861 for the LNWR, the first work on which he was joined by his nephew. Charles Liddell was the engineer for this line, one of many contracts where Liddell and Firbank worked together in forty years of joint activity. Charles Liddell next became a consultant engineer on the Midland Railway's Southern Extension Committee, which advised and checked the progress of the line from Bedford to St Pancras. Firbank bid for and gained contract Nos 2 and 3 from near Kentish Town to just short of the Brent Viaduct. To the north of him were the Waring Brothers and beyond them Brassey and Ballard. The engineer in charge was William Barlow, whose section included the heavy earthworks and tunnelling needed to build the line around the southern edge of Hampstead Heath. Once started, the major part of the work was done in eighteen months, with continuous day and night work to complete the Belsize tunnels, enabling goods trains to be run earlier than expected into the new goods station. At the peak of building activity in 1866, Firbank employed nearly 2,000 men. His reputation to take over the failures of others was recalled when Waring Brothers gave up their No 4 contract towards the end of 1866, when financial pressures were too hot even for them. Firbank now had his nephew Ralph and his seventeen-year-old son Joseph Thomas with him, so he took over the Warings' work and actually started to catch up on the backlog, despite the heavy nature of the work on Brent Viaduct and Elstree Tunnel. By accepting shares from the Midland Railway, against his usual practice, he was able to keep going in that year of crisis when others failed and had now proved himself able to take on the largest contracts.

Thus it was that Firbank had no difficulty in obtaining No 3 contract from the Midland Railway on its formidable Settle–Carlisle line. His section from Smardale to Newbiggin included the tunnels at Crosby Garrett and Helm, but it was by no means the most arduous section of the line. He obtained access to it via the Stockton & Darlington line at Appleby. There he constructed a hutted encampment, which moved as the works required. Shops, hospital, reading room and coffee houses were available to the men once the town was too distant for easy access, the last named being an attempt to keep the men sober. This endeavour did not always succeed as the local constabulary once seized kegs of ale from the camp, though not supplied by Firbank, whose idea of a treat for the men was oatmeal, barley water and meat. Despite his own agnosticism, Firbank brought in a clergyman to improve the morals of the men.

Firbank's original tender had been for £278,813 for the 14½ miles of line. The ferocious weather, access difficulties over execrable local roads and the high turnover of labour which resulted in demands for double rates from the navvies, all increased costs to the point where the contractors considered getting out. The contractor of No 1 contract, Ashwell, builder of St Pancras, in fact relinquished his contract to the Midland Railway, but Firbank stuck it out, his other works forming a protective barrier when things went wrong. Firbank obtained further work constructing intermediate stations and other works at Appleby, including making a junction with the North Eastern Railway, thus partly compensating for earlier losses. The Midland board must have appreciated Firbank's sticking to the job because they gave him the Birmingham West Suburban Railway contract in 1883 where he had to rebuild an existing line through an urbanised area up to main line standards.

The other railways with which Joseph Firbank worked were the Great Northern Railway from 1869 to 1878, doing much of the widening work on the lines out of King's Cross, including the new Copenhagen Tunnel. Much of their penetrating line from Nottingham to Burton on Trent was also his. The Somers Town Goods Depot for the Midland Railway was a masterpiece of brickwork, built in his last years, mostly under the direction of his son who was taking an increasing part of the work-load from his father. Ralph Firbank left the firm in 1877 to start his own contracting business, his major work being the GN&GE Joint Railway from Spalding to Lincoln. His promising independent career was cut short after starting to build extensively in South Africa. An apoplectic fit killed him in December 1882 at the age of forty-six.

The final contract on which father and son were engaged was the Bournemouth Direct Line for the London & South Western Railway from Brockenhurst to Christchurch. Old Joseph saw little of the work as he was ailing badly by the time that the contract started. Indeed his connection with the LSWR dated only from 1883 when the firm had recently moved from Newport to London Bridge. The contract although short, some 8½ miles, was one of the most difficult undertaken by the firm. The previous contractors had abandoned it, finding the greatest difficulties with the clay of the Headon and Barton beds, a greasy substance that gives rise to constant landslips. The sands and gravels of the area are also bad railway earthwork material, being extremely porous and liable to run in heavy rain. With true Firbank grit, the contract was fulfilled despite all obstacles. A sub-contractor on this line was John Mowlem, founder of the great contracting firm. Like others now active, he gained his first experience with the great railway contractors of the late nineteenth century.

Father and son rarely see eye to eye on everything, especially when in business together. So it was with the Firbanks. Old Joseph was a genius at building railways, had a calculating mind that needed no elaborate machinery to check the results and worked hard and long all his life, devoting more time to his public services than his business in his later years. The other side was an intolerance towards leisure, foreigners and paper deals. Although the son was sent to Cheltenham College for his education, father could not get used to the habits he had picked up there. When visiting a site under his son's charge, he noted a hunting horse tethered among the work horses in the stables, remarking that the hunter 'woarn't pull a load o' muck'. When he built a railway across St Pancras churchyard, the French Catholic authorities required for reburial the bones of a bishop buried there while a refugee from the French Revolution. The navvies had already started work, scattering the bones, so when he had to assemble likely skeletons, Firbank chose the darkest set of bones he could find, reasoning that all foreigners were dark! One story is that he even refused a contract in the Isle of Wight because that was abroad, while Ireland and overseas contracts were not even considered. Old Joseph did good work at a fair price for hard cash, and by and large his son followed these principles, allowing himself only the indulgence of building a line into Ventnor, Isle of Wight.

Young Joseph Firbank married a vicar's daughter from Ireland, acquired a family mansion in Chislehurst and a house in the West End, started collecting *objets d'art* and paintings, and in 1895 followed so many other railway contractors by becoming an MP, in this case Tory member for Hull East, retaining it without any marked distinction until the Tory rout of 1906. His list of speeches in *Hansard* is short indeed, one on a West Indian problem. Despite his move to London, he followed his father as Deputy Lieutenant of Monmouthshire and also became High Sheriff.

Charles Liddell still continued to parcel out work to the Firbanks. He did much work for the Metropolitan Railway, which was being extended to the north west of London. The Harrow extension was built by the Firbanks in 1878–80, then the extension northwards to Aylesbury. Work for the LBSCR line from Oxted to Groombridge kept the firm close to London, where they were in an excellent position to tender for the Manchester, Sheffield & Lincolnshire Railway's London extension, getting Marylebone passenger and goods stations, the coal yard in Grove Road (now Lisson Grove) and also a contract to build 4½ acres of barrack-like blocks of flats built to replace 37 acres of houses demolished to provide room for the new terminus. Wharncliffe Gardens, as they were known, were named after the chairman of the MSLR (renamed the Great Central Railway to reflect its new aspirations).

The largest single contract of the entry into London was No 7, from Canfield Place to Marylebone. Charles Liddell was engineer to the Metropolitan Railway up to his death in 1894, so was concerned with the initial planning of the junction with the new line. The Metropolitan Railway gave access to contract No 7, being the main entry route for machinery and materials as well as the chief means of disposing of the mountains of spoil created by the massive demolition and tunnelling operations.

Work started on the Wharncliffe Gardens site in the early autumn of 1895 in order to rehouse the people to be displaced by demolition. First the house of the artist Edwin Landseer had to be demolished, then the gardens leading down to the Regent's Canal were filled in and a gigantic retaining wall erected so that flats could be built almost to the water's edge. There were 325 flats with two rooms, 165 flats with three rooms and a mere 50 with four rooms. Although model dwellings by contemporary working-class standards, they were a telling example of the overcrowding that was tolerable to the MSLR directors and their class. Up to ten people lived in each of these flats. Yet solid they undoubtedly were in the best Firbank tradition of massive brick construction. A direct hit by a V1 'doodle bug' on 21 August 1944 brought down only the actual stairways that it hit, leaving the structure of other blocks only yards away virtually undamaged.

Work on the demolition of the main Marylebone site was able to start in May 1896. Tunnelling under Lord's cricket ground had to wait until the end of August and the finish of the cricket season, so that the ground, enlarged and improved at railway expense, would not have its season interfered with. Then the contractors had to finish the tunnel by May 1897 before the start of the next season. About 3,000 men worked a full six-day week for over two years on the Marylebone sites, aided by 23 steam cranes, 6 portable engines and a steam navvy. The work on the cramped site was still largely manual – hence the numbers. The steam cranes only helped with the loading. Sunday was never worked as this was St John's Wood.

This line was the climax of the main-line building era as far as London was concerned. Three tunnels, massive bridges over the LNWR at Hampstead, bridging and embanking of the Regent's Canal, made it an impressive and expensive exercise. The son of the young ex-miner who urged his gang on in Woodhead Tunnel was now negotiating directly with the directors of that railway in its greatly enlarged form.

J. T. Firbank went on to receive his knighthood shortly after the completion of the GCR into London. He executed a few more contracts, including the improvement of the northern section of the Midland & South Western Junction Railway from Cirencester to Andoversford at the turn of the century, but this was small beer after the great contracts of former years. Profits were slimmer and Sir Thomas seemed to have lost his magic touch. His eldest boy died, leaving Ronald Firbank as heir to what was left of the family fortune when Sir Thomas died in 1910. Ronald was an aesthete and a novelist with no wish to carry on the family business. One link with the past survives: a relative runs a contracting business in Luton, mainly concerned with waste disposal!

The Firbanks were the alternative model of how to conduct a railway contracting business. Had all the railways been able to raise cash and employ contractors like the Firbanks, undoubtedly much less money would have been spent and many of the financial problems would have been avoided. As it was, only solvent railways could afford to employ them, although the quality of their work probably made them the best buy in the end.

Considerably larger than Firbanks in total size because they did not stop at railway contracting were the three firms that comprised the Lucas & Aird partnership. The partnership had started in the tradition of shifting alliances typical of the 1860s, but in 1870 it was formalised into three firms: Lucas & Aird was the main railway contracting arm of the business, John Aird & Sons dealt largely with gas and water construction, while Lucas Brothers were more concerned with public and general building. The split in function also reflected the desire in the wake of the 1866 crisis to protect the partners in case of the failure of any one large contract. Should one arm of the partnership fail, two would still be left. The two principal partners were Charles Lucas, who had had building businesses in Norwich and Lowestoft and had been one of Peto's many partners before he became independent, and the younger John Aird, who inherited his father's gas and water contracting business in London in 1870, one that supplied cities with their public utilities in many parts of the world. Thomas Lucas, later knighted, and Alfred Lucas were the least active partners of the four.

During construction of the Metropolitan District Railway under the Thames Embankment, John Aird had built the lengthy lower tunnel which took London's sewage from west to east, while Lucas built the railway and Charing Cross Station above the sewage. The diarist A. J. Munby lived in the Temple in 1864, during construction. His view was 'outlined by the scaffold beams and dredging engines ranged far out in the river opposite; whilst above the steamboat pier, acres of made land appear above high water, shapeless and slovenly. And the old steps of the Temple stairs have been carried off to make way for the monster.' He did not refrain from using the monster once opened, however. Lucas was also an experienced tunneller, being engaged with Brassey and Wythes on the East London Railway and having built the Norwich waterworks; his business complemented as well as overlapped Aird's. They were jointly engaged on extending the fledgling underground system by building the Hammersmith & City line and the Metropolitan and St John's Wood Railway. The Lucas brothers themselves were fully engaged in building Liverpool Street Station and hotel in the mid-1870s as well as in completing much of Peto's unfinished work on the LCDR lines once that unfortunate railway was in a position to pay again for work done.

Charles Lucas built up an excellent reputation in London, but his work for the East Norfolk Railway, just a little side show as far as such a large firm was concerned, left much to be desired. He inherited a line that had been barely started by a previous contractor, William Smith Simpson, who had died in 1867. The idea was to build first from Norwich to North Walsham and extend onwards to Cromer, where it was hoped to develop a major resort, 'another Scarborough' in the words of Charles Parkes, director of the Great Eastern Railway. Lucas spoke to the local landowner, Lord Suffield, about the prospects for erecting hotels and apartments there; he always seemed to be on the look-out for further work. Construction was slow, it badly missed the deadline for opening in May 1874 and was an indirect cause of the Thorpe disaster when two trains collided head-on while running on a single line track in September 1874. Next to that single track was a second track whose opening had been delayed by Lucas's tardiness. Even when the line was opened the following month, no goods trains were able to run during the busiest season because facilities had not been installed. Level crossing keepers' houses had not been erected, so a kind of sentry box was used and to cap it all, Lucas exceeded his estimate and then had the nerve to offer to extend the line to Cromer. His offer was turned down. The East Norfolk board had had enough of contractors and decided to do the job themselves.

Lucas & Aird usually undertook grand contracts. Their other major contracts included Tilbury and London docks, the Hull & Barnsley Railway, the West Highland Railway, the Manton to Kettering line for the Midland Railway with two long tunnels and the magnificent Welland Viaduct of eighty-two arches as well as the Rhondda & Swansea Bay Railway, all considerably larger than the puny East Norfolk Railway. They also built extensively overseas. Their dock work and railway work fitted neatly together with the advent of the great railway-cum-dock schemes of the late nineteenth century, when much larger steamships needed larger docks and plentiful supplies of coal, while the mines were expanding fast and exporting their surplus through new docks and ports specially built for the purpose.

The Hull & Barnsley Railway was such a concept; the new Alexandra Dock at Hull was combined with a railway penetrating the Yorkshire coalfield, a massive operation which was completed in the four years up to 1885. The total cost of the railway and docks was over £6m, more than twice the original estimate, which left the Hull & Barnsley a financial cripple, trying to pay off massive debts for many years afterwards. For Lucas & Aird the line was one of the biggest single projects attempted up to that time, involving tunnelling, deep cuttings and the excavation by steam power of one of the largest docks built to date. Despite some considerable mechanical aids, the number of navvies employed was often between 5,000 and 8,000, gathering in East Yorkshire from the whole of the British Isles. They lived in hutted camps, a trade that Lucas had earlier made a speciality, crowded but much less so than in earlier times and with some discipline asserted by the ganger and his wife who were in charge of each hut. Other similar work followed on the Rhondda & Swansea Bay Railway, but on a much smaller scale.

One of the least successful of Lucas's ventures was the Alexandra Palace in which he was largely partnered by his colleague of Metropolitan days, Sir John Kelk. The idea was to give north London a similar vast hall and pleasure park to south London's Crystal Palace, complete with railways serving it, in this case the Great Northern and, in 1878, the Great Eastern. A vast brick hall for organ recitals and exhibitions was erected, but burnt down only a few days later. It was re-erected but was never economically successful, although later serving as the first television headquarters and then the Open University's television studio. It was again burned down in 1980. Despite such setbacks, Lucas & Aird were never in the danger of bankruptcy that their forebears were, having taken much trouble to cover themselves.

Charles Lucas tended to become more of a country squire in the 1880s at his Sussex estate, Warnham Court. In politics, although often invited to stand, he preferred to be a consultant rather than an active member, advising Disraeli and W. H. Smith on labour matters. It was thus left to John Aird to tender successfully for the West Highland Railway contract from Craigendoran to Fort William, 100 miles of the roughest country in Britain. For Aird it was a return to his father's roots, almost a pious duty for an *émigré* Scot trying to revive the Highlands that his father and grandfather had been forced to abandon in the early years of the century. Although a lengthy line, requiring some 5,000 navvies to work on the different sections at any one time, the lump sum contract for £393,683 4s 2d also meant that it was a cheap line. When the going was tougher than expected, a quarrel between contractors and board resulted in the contractors downing tools until granted an extra £10,000 on the contract. John Aird was not making a present of the contract to the Highlands, despite a preference for employing local labour. The extension of the line to Mallaig required a government guarantee to safeguard the finances, but this was not immediately forthcoming, so Lucas & Aird's hopes of continuing the line were in vain, although they seem to have been ready to start in the autumn of 1894, just as they had been at North Walsham two decades previously. Charles Lucas died on 4 December 1895 'from general decay' as his obituarist put it, but John Aird, knighted and active almost to the end, built dams and railways in Egypt early in the new century, vastly increasing the irrigated area of the Nile Valley below Aswan, where he had constructed the first and second dams. Earlier he had been disappointed by the way in which the Manchester Ship Canal contract had gone to Thomas Walker and by the growth of Weetman Pearson's contracting firm, which had eclipsed his own, dominant since the 1870s; but his second wind, at an age when most others would have been thinking of retirement, also included the expansion of Bristol's docks, the Avonmouth Royal Edward Dock and many smaller jobs. He died on 6 January 1911, his last years darkened by the failure of his sons to complete a large contract for the construction of docks in Singapore. The ploy that had worked on the West Highland Railway two decades before, of stopping work to obtain an upward revision, no longer produced the desired results. Machinery and site were seized, followed by a legal battle and the loss of £1m by the firm. It was a sad end, but few contractors have had really successful heirs.

John Aird had a busy public life, being the first mayor of Paddington, an active member of the Railway Staff Corps which was so important in the reconquest of the Sudan in 1898 when he was working at Aswan. Politically he was chiefly remembered as MP for North Paddington from 1887 to 1905; he was joined in the Commons by fellow contractor MPs Sir Thomas Firbank and Weetman Pearson. In addition to this, John Aird also knew how to enjoy life to the full. He had theatrical companies come to his London residence to give performances, while his country seat, Wilton Park at Beaconsfield, provided him with leisure and relaxation in periods when he was not driving a contract to a speedy and usually successful conclusion.

Both Charles Lucas and John Aird were hard and domineering individuals who worked well together despite quarrels with other relatives in the family firms and between themselves. The relatives were used to superintending work on widely separated contracts, Alfred Lucas on the Hull & Barnsley, the Aird sons in Singapore and so on. Lucas & Aird's chief contribution was to bring together a wide variety of expertise necessary for the increasing complexity of railway, dock and city construction, which were often strongly interlinked. They had the technical ability and capital strength to carry through any job that the period offered when it was technically possible. Few could match them in tendering for the most complex jobs until almost the end of the century.

Weetman Pearson was the third generation of a small provincial contracting company, S. Pearson & Son, which was originally founded in Bradford and had done local railway work for the Lancashire & Yorkshire Railway and the Great Northern Railway for some two decades before the founder's grandson was old enough to supervise contracts himself and make decisions that he could carry against his weak but affable father. His first big contract was the King's Lynn Docks & Railway Company in 1879–84, taken for £105,000; it was the firm's first outside the north. The estimate had been cut to the bone to obtain it, but combined with the nearby Ipswich Main Drainage Scheme at £60,000 and much hard work, including driving his own traction engine as well as taking his share of the navvying, the young Pearson made the jobs profitable and himself independent to the extent that on completion of the King's Lynn contract, he moved the firm from Bradford to London. In the next five years he moved from being a small but successful new arrival to being one of the major contractors in the land. New docks at Southampton, Milford Haven and Halifax, Nova Scotia, tripled the size of contracts that he took on, preparing him for the great leap of taking on the Avila & Salamanca Railway for nearly £1m in Spain, and a series of railway, drainage and later oil, power and tramway contracts in Mexico, that took him to the top of the world contracting league. He was one of the few European contractors ever to be successful in the USA where he first did work on the Hudson Tunnel in 1889–95, going on in 1904 to make the East River tunnels for the Long Island Railroad at a cost of £3½m. The Blackwall Tunnel under the Thames confirmed his reputation as one of a new breed of tunnellers, working with the Greathead shield and compressed air to perform hitherto impossible feats of construction. In a quarter of a century up to 1900 he had made a profit on every contract undertaken. His careful calculation, good labour relations and the enormous care that he took to see that his men were well housed and protected against tropical diseases and other hazards, made him an employer who could always rely on getting the quality and quantity of labour that he wanted. By the turn of the century this was a necessary attribute, given his huge work-load.

A list that Pearson made out for his son at the turn of the century, who was acting as an assistant, contained some fourteen works, nine of them in Britain, two in Ireland, the remainder in Mexico and China, involving 19,500 men employed and worth some £12m. Six of the works were railways, including one of the early tube lines – the Great Northern & City Railway, while

Navvy huts on the Great Central Railway at Helmdon Road in North-amptonshire in 1897 (*from the collection of S.W.A. Newton and by permission of Leicestershire Museums, Art Galleries and Records Service*)

The derailment of one of William Mouseley's spoil wagons on the Norfolk & Suffolk Joint Railways in 1898. The locomotive is a Manning Wardle 0–6–0T, although the connecting rods to the front wheels have been disconnected (*Shaw Collection*)

Sir Joseph Firbank's 0–6–0ST *Newport*, built by Hunslet of Leeds in 1876, at Marylebone in 1897 (*from the collection of S.W.A. Newton and by permission of Leicestershire Museums, Art Galleries and Records Service*)

By the turn of the century, mechanisation was making a material difference to construction. Mechanical plant can be seen here assisting in the construction of the station and cattle docks at Fishguard in 1907 (*National Museum of Wales*)

docks and waterworks formed the remainder of the business. The change that had come about in the firm which twenty years before had considered £105,000 its biggest contract to date is emphasised by Pearson's note on the Ross & Wicklow Railway contract, worth £100,000, classed as 'a railway some 12 or 16 miles long, I forget which, of no particular difficulty or importance'. Pearson had reached the position where he could chat over the possibilities of a railway from Athens to Larissa with the King of Greece, or make honest bargains with the President of Mexico on a man-to-man basis. His refusal to offer bribes impressed the Mexicans and led to many concessions, including the Tehuantepec Railway and associated harbours on the Atlantic and Pacific shores, Mexico's answer to the Panama Canal then being built, and today being rebuilt to serve its original purpose on a larger scale.

The overseas contracts did not lead to abandonment of British interests. For the Great Western Railway, he widened the line from Plympton to Brent, taking part in the gauge conversion of that line in 1892. A small job in 1896 was the speedy ten months' construction of the Lambourn Valley Light Railway from Newbury, while also making the original line for the Port Talbot Railway & Dock Company, one of several Welsh coal carriers making integrated railways and docks during the great coal export boom. The same boom generated the South Wales Direct line of the Great Western Railway, a truly major undertaking linking the new Severn Tunnel with Swindon to avoid the congested Bristol area. The 33½ miles were let at £1,300,000 for a well-graded double main line, the Chipping Sodbury Tunnel, some 2½ miles in length, and two others, major viaducts and earthworks as well as complex junctions at Filton and Yate. The problems came with the Chipping Sodbury Tunnel, which was estimated to be a dry tunnel but a spring proved so intractable that another tunnel under the trackbed had to be constructed to carry the excess water away. The result was that the line cost Pearson some £1,612,000 and of course no profit after six years of work. An attempt to get redress from the GWR failed, despite an award to Pearson under the arbitration of no less an engineer than Sir Benjamin Baker. Legal proceedings likewise failed, resulting in Pearson refusing to work again for the GWR, whose position was that problems of this sort were part of the risk undertaken by a contractor. The Midland Railway was more generous to Thomas Oliver, who was reimbursed for additional work on the contemporary Totley Tunnel.

Most of Pearson's work was for payment as work was done, but he did invest heavily in the Great Northern & City tube railway as well as guaranteeing 3 per cent dividend on the stock that he did not own. It was an unusual tube in that it could take standard rolling stock, an advantage exploited recently when the Great Northern suburban lines were electrified. Pearson took over from a failed contractor and pushed the project hard, but was unable to interest the Great Northern Railway itself in running trains over the new line, so he continued to work it despite its lack of profitability until its incorporation in the underground group.

One other railway project that Pearson undertook was out of the ordinary – the Lancashire, Derbyshire & East Coast Railway. Like the Hull & Barnsley, the Port Talbot and several others, it sought to link a developing coalfield with a new dock, in this case Mablethorpe, which was never built, but also to cross the Pennines to supply coal-hungry Lancashire and have another port on the Manchester Ship Canal at Warrington. The Midland Railway built another line across the Pennines from Sheffield to Manchester shortly afterwards, so there was no impossible vision about the scheme, just the limitations of finance which dogged so many independent ventures. The core of the system was the line from Lincoln to Chesterfield, a contract largely made by Pearson who established his headquarters near Warsop. Brickyards, a locomotive shed for eight contractor's engines, blacksmithy, carpenters' shop, workmen's club, dispensary for the sick and a better class of accommodation for the navvies than hitherto seen made this a model construction site. He followed through his Liberal convictions by paying piece-work rates, but with a guaranteed minimum, and then giving a bonus when profits were adequate. Social welfare for the men through the Navvies' Mission Society and the Aged Navvies' Pension Fund, of which his wife was treasurer and president, indicated his concern for his men. In return he obtained the good and prompt completion of most of his contracts. Sub-contracting became less important, the age of the professional manager and engineers employed by the contractor had arrived. Thus the LDECR was completed in five years as Pearson's first home £1m contract.

In the twentieth century there were few home railway contracts, so Pearson took water, harbour, factory and coal-mining contracts, acquired a peerage with the title of Lord Cowdray and established his family firm in a wide variety of activities which after his death dropped the contracting business.

The Firbanks, Lucas & Aird and Pearson are but a few of the major contracting companies of the late Victorian period, but they were the ones most heavily involved in building or remodelling the railways. Other great companies included, for instance, Logan & Hemingway, whose work for the Great Central Railway included docks, as well as the No 1 contract on the London Extension. One of the principals, John W. Logan, was an MP. The firm was started by the Hemingway brothers, masons to the Nowells in the 1830s, who formed the company in 1865. The firm became highly mechanised during the last decades of the nineteenth century. Its locomotive fleet is the subject of a later chapter. Henry Lovatt of Wolverhampton, Thomas Oliver of Rugby and Walter Scott of Newcastle all had contracts from the GCR and were prominent in tendering for other lines being built in East Anglia, South Wales, the Midlands and the North East.

The very last main-line system to be built, the Great Western & Great Central Joint Railway and its extensions, joining Old Oak Common in London, to Aynho near Banbury, was contracted right through the reign of Edward VII, 1901–10. R. W. Pauling & Co had a major contract from Northolt to High Wycombe, nearly 17 miles of moderately hilly ground. They attacked it with no less than 16 steam excavators, carried away the spoil in 895 trucks, hauled by 34 locomotives, which were stabled at Gerrards Cross. The other contractors of the system were equally mechanised for the period, but this did not appear to speed the works in comparison with the times of earlier manual contracts. The section from Ashenden to Aynho through generally easily worked Jurassic rocks took four years under Messrs Scott & Middleton. The Great Northern Railway was also active at this time with the Hertford Loop and Midville cut-off.

Thereafter, railway work for major contractors was fitful and forthcoming only when funds permitted, usually at the Government's behest in time of war and depression. A few minor branch lines and connections remained to be built, marshalling yards consolidated and remodelled, some lines were widened or electrified in the inter-war period, but it was hand-to-mouth work, gratefully accepted but not the stuff of which livelihoods are made. The period from World War I until the modernisation programme of the late 1950s can be regarded as one of make-do-and-mend in terms of railway contracting.

8
Skills and Interests

Railway contractors came from diverse backgrounds and developed a wide variety of skills; some like bridging and tunnelling, excavating and infilling, were applicable to a much wider variety of jobs than railway construction. The great bridge builders and tunnellers such as Fairbairn, Arrol and Walker were so distinctive as to require separate treatment. They did their most spectacular work for the railways, but it was always part of a much wider engineering interest.

Successful railway contractors found that their acquired skills were of wider application. The Crystal Palace was one of the first demonstrations of what they could achieve in a non-rail context. Later work in coal mining, oil drilling, dock and canal construction indelibly showed the transferability of these skills to the wider interests that the greatest railway contractors usually manifested. Their interest in politics likewise continued into the present century.

Simple culverts and bridges of traditional pattern in brick, stone or timber could be built by local contractors under the supervision of the engineer or his agent. The more adventurous engineering demanded by the lines sanctioned in the Railway Mania period produced a need for specialist knowledge which constantly pushed the frontiers of construction further forward. Experiments with cast and wrought iron indicated that there was a future for these materials in the construction of large bridges which were needed to cross the wide waterways which blocked direct routes along the coast of North Wales or along the east coast of Scotland.

The first specialist railway bridge builder to emerge was William Fairbairn who, unlike so many of the young lions of the railway era, was over fifty years of age and full of experience in related fields before he started to build bridges for the new railways in the 1840s. His career had started in 1803 at the age of fourteen in colliery engineering. Work on the earliest steamboats captured his attention, as well as bridge building, millwrighting and the construction of mill buildings, using wrought iron in increasing quantities to lighten the structures. As late as 1817, when he built the Blackfriars Bridge in Manchester, he was still a humble and poorly lettered journeyman, but was starting to employ others on a larger scale. He anticipated the Victorian paradigm of workman to boss when he wrote that 'the examples of Franklin, Ferguson and Watt were always before me and though I laboured under great difficulties as regards education, and had little time at my disposal for study, nevertheless I so far imitated their example as to be able to go on cheerfully and enthusiastically in my endeavours to be useful and my determination to excel'. Fairbairn opened two factories, one on the Thames at Millwall, the other in Manchester, where he produced wrought iron for construction and machinery. When Robert Stephenson was seeking ways of bridging the Conway and Menai waterways for the Chester & Holyhead Railway in 1845, Fairbairn was a natural choice. The two men conducted experiments at the Millwall yard 'to determine the details and properties of the colossal wrought iron tubular bridges to be erected on the Chester & Holyhead Railway'. Great care was taken to see that there was no likelihood of bridge collapse, as Fairbairn wrote to Stephenson on 6 August 1845:

> From these investigations we derive several important facts, one of which I may mention, namely the difficulty in bringing the upper as well as the lower side of the bridge into tensile strain. For this object several changes were effected, and attempts were made to distribute the forces equally, or in certain proportion throughout the parts but without effect, the results being in every experiment that of a hollow beam or girder, resisting in the usual way by the compression of the upper and the extension of the lower sides. In almost every instance we have found the resistance opposed to compression the weakest: the upper side generally giving way from the severity of the strain in that direction.

Experiments continued in the following year, aided by the mathematician Mr Eaton Hodgkinson, so that by April 1846 they could proceed from models to actual construction. Fairbairn was appointed 'to superintend construction, to appoint all persons necessary, furnish a list of persons required to the directors, together with a list of salaries, foremen and others above the class of workmen and to submit money required for works with payment on production of certificates from the engineer together with accounts and vouchers'. The result was the triumphant erection of two great and long-lasting bridges, aesthetically pleasing as well as functional, which gave Fairbairn an international reputation.

Although Fairbairn was able to work successfully to the highest standards of the time, his lack of education was still against him. When he was invited to address the Institute of Civil Engineers in 1849, he had the help of friends in penning the final result and in giving the statistics which were *de rigueur* on such occasions. The intuitive genius was not the image that was presentable.

As was the case with Thomas Brassey, offers from overseas arrived once Fairbairn's fame had been established at home. He constructed the Hohenzollern Bridge across the Rhine at Cologne, with a rigid design that allowed headroom for the busy waterway traffic below. He was later received by the King of Prussia and the great scientists Alexander von Humboldt and Baron Bunsen. Such overseas acclaim paved the way for his acceptance in the highest strata of British scientific society when he was made a Fellow of the Royal Society. The Athenaeum Club made him a member without a ballot, adding a rare distinction to a growing list.

Meanwhile Fairbairn brought his sons further into the business, working on high-pressure steam boilers for ships, and by developing his ideas for tubular bridges so that standard items could be manufactured in quantity. Between 1846 and 1851 he had erected over 100 lengths varying from 40ft to 180ft. In the next two decades, this figure was multiplied tenfold, using over 100,000 tons of wrought iron, made to exacting standards. Other work, much of it for the railways, included the manufacture of girders, cranes, roofs and caissons. The dome of the Royal Albert Hall and the great suite of mills for Salts of Saltaire are also the work of Fairbairns. The Fairbairn yards at Millwall were closed down in the depression following the Railway Mania, but later reopened by Brunel and Scott Russell for the construction of the *Great Eastern*. The highly profitable Fairbairn works at Canal Street, Manchester, continued in production until the 1870s, largely under the sons after 1853, while the elder Fairbairn was on call as a valued consultant until his death in 1874.

William Fairbairn thus instituted the pattern of specialist bridge building in which engineer and contractor plan the bridge, whose parts are then made in a specialist works and brought to the site for erection by employees of the contractor. In three decades, Fairbairns made over 1,000 bridges. Brassey and Peto's Canada Works at Birkenhead followed the pattern with usually good results. The dominance of these companies was eclipsed by the 1870s, so that the construction of the first Tay Bridge was passed by default to a succession of less experienced contractors, the first two of whom relinquished the contract, being succeeded by Hopkins, Gilkes & Co of Middlesbrough, locomotive and civil engineers, whose Belah and Deepdale viaducts on the line from Tebay to Barnard Castle, were landmarks in the Pennines until the early 1960s. They were designed by Sir Thomas Bouch, who brought Hopkins, Gilkes & Co to Scotland to build his ill-fated Tay Bridge.

The story of Sir Thomas Bouch's Tay Bridge is well known, but the part that the contractors played bears repetition, as it formed an unpleasant coda between the honest and substantial work of the pioneering Fairbairn and the later work of Sir William Arrol, his natural successor in adventurous bridge building in the age of steel. The first Tay Bridge was a hybrid of brick, stone, cast and wrought iron. The most defective features seem to have been the cast-iron parts manufactured on the banks of the Tay, where salt water was used to damp the moulding sand. Poor castings were used, lacking brackets and lugs, and some had cracks in them before they were erected. These were tarted up for inspection with a mixture of soot and wax known as Beaumont's Egg. Sections of the bridge fitted badly but were nevertheless joined together more in hope than full confidence. Slack inspection by foreman and engineer alike, followed by slack maintenance when the bridge was in use, led to disaster like some inevitable Greek tragedy. The 1870s were bad years for the railways as far as safety was concerned, more intensive services were being run without commensurate improvements in braking and signalling, resulting in a number of sensational accidents and increasing death and injury to staff. Matters improved thereafter.

William Arrol was very much in the mould of William Fairbairn, although born some two generations later. He trained as a blacksmith, attending evening classes and reading books to repair the huge gaps in his education. By the age of twenty he had become a foreman at the engineering works of Messrs Laidlaw in Glasgow, getting his first large-scale experience in erecting Deal Pier in 1865 and Brighton West Pier in the following year. The company also did some railway bridgework. Young Arrol set up his own rival company in 1868 and, despite his extreme youth, obtained the Caledonian Railway contract to build the great bridge across the Clyde from Glasgow Central Station to the Gorbals. Work also came from the North British Railway, with whom he had a very long and useful association.

The North British plan for a direct route from Edinburgh to Aberdeen involved the building of the Forth Bridge, in addition to the ill-fated first Tay Bridge. The Bouch design for the Forth Bridge was left in abeyance after 1879, so that by the time the NBR considered the new design by Benjamin Baker, the relatively new medium of steel had been developed to the point where it could be used both for that and the new Tay Bridge. By the early 1880s, William Arrol had sufficient experience and capital to tender for both bridges. Much of the work was pioneering, for no similar work of steel had been completed elsewhere in a narrow estuary where the type of storm that had destroyed the Tay Bridge was a commonplace, with the added hazard that the Forth Bridge structure was 400ft high. Arrol was simultaneously engaged on the replacement Tay Bridge, completing it in 1887, nearly three years before the Forth Bridge. The quality of material this time and the inspection procedures ensured that there was no repeat of the 1879 disaster. The Forth Bridge later became the model for the even more daring Quebec Bridge across the St Lawrence. A lighter note was struck by Arrol's building of Tower Bridge in London. He was also a considerable industrialist, with a large works at Dalmarnock giving his inventiveness an outlet. He gained a knighthood thanks to his sterling work on the Forth Bridge, ending his days in 1913 as the grand old man of Scottish engineering, head of the firm that made cars at a time when Walter Chrysler was still working for the Chicago Great Western Railway. A link with the past during the construction of the Forth and Tay bridges was that Sir James Falshaw, Brassey's old partner, was now the chairman of the North British Railway which gave Arrol his greatest opportunity.

Arrol's other major Scottish cantilever bridge was the Connel Ferry Bridge on the Caledonian Railway's Ballachulish branch, built in the early years of this century. The approaches and stonework were built by the main contractors for the branch, Best & Co of Edinburgh. Arrol's specialist team of erectors and riveters were indispensable in this tricky work and travelled worldwide on their many contracts. The testing of the Connel Ferry Bridge was carried out by a load of 740 tons crossing it, including eight locomotives, a test which it passed with flying colours.

The Waddell family of Edinburgh were chiefly remembered for the building of the Mersey rail tunnel, only just a precursor of the more famous Severn Tunnel, but in its time a magnificent piece of pioneering. The construction took six years from 1880–6, with Charles Fox's sons and James Brunlees as engineers. Although attempts had been made to tunnel under the Severn and the English Channel when the project started, neither had succeeded, so this was the longest underwater tunnel completed up to 1886. Nearly a mile of it was actually under the Mersey and much of the rock through which the tunnel was driven was cracked or porous, including a former lower bed of the Mersey itself. Thus, in addition to the rail tunnel, drainage tunnels had to be built sloping down to massive sumps, from which 8,000 gallons of water per minute had to be pumped to the surface. One of the greatest fears of the miners was that they would break through the bed of the Mersey and drown, but they were reassured by Francis Fox's visits to them at 3.00am to demonstrate his solicitude. He bored 2in diameter holes upwards from the tunnel with a 15ft drill, never piercing the river bed, so he was always able to reassure the tunnellers that they had a good thickness above them. Fortunately there was great faith in the engineer's pronouncements. Although inspection was rigorous and great care was taken by the contractors and engineers alike to prevent accidents, the human element caused one of the more serious accidents on this lengthy and difficult contract:

At Liverpool, at 4 o'clock one morning, when the 'shifts' were changing, some young miners in the lift cage, eight in number, who were descending the shaft began 'sky-larking'. When the cage was about half way down, one of them let his petroleum lamp project beyond the edge of the cage. The lamp was caught by the shaft timbers and upset, with the result that the petroleum flowed all over the bottom of the cage, and there was immediately a bonfire with eight men in it. Hearing the noise and cries of the men, the engine-man at 'bank' stopped the cage, which was consequently suspended halfway down the shaft. Two of the men jumped out, and falling to the bottom, were instantly killed, two others climbed up the wire rope to get out of the flames, and the other four were badly burnt.[1]

New methods were contrasted with old on this contract. The men in the accident were going down to work manually with hand drills and explosives and making painfully slow progress of only 4½ft per working day, whereas on the Birkenhead face, a Beaumont power drill was at work which could advance 32ft in a day. However, like most new machinery, its reliability was poor, so that both faces had advanced the same distance when they met, a mere inch out of alignment. Waddell had no problems finding either men or accommodation for them with large towns on both banks of the river. The round-the-clock blasting by Waddell while tunnelling from Liverpool to Birkenhead had a bizarre consequence when the Grand Fleet was at anchor in the Mersey above the tunnel. Underwater explosions made the Admiral think that he had been torpedoed. Full alert was sounded, sailors roused from their hammocks, all doors below decks were closed and a full examination was carried out, with no result. Only in the cold light of day was it discovered that the tunnel was the cause of the imagined attempt to blow up the fleet.

Waddell had built several small- to medium-sized lines in

Scotland and was simultaneously engaged on several lines in East
Anglia for the Great Eastern, where he executed contract after
contract with prompt, reasonably priced work which passed
Board of Trade inspection first time. His other main field of
endeavour was in mining, which eventually provided the family
with its investment mainstay, the Great Mountain mine on the
Llanelly & Mynydd Mawr Railway which the Waddells ran.
They also built an iron ore railway on the North York Moors
known as Paddy Waddell's Railway, that being his nickname. His
investment interests included the Rosewell Gas Company,
Burntisland Oil Company (which mined and refined oil shale)
and Northern Cable Tramways, forerunners of electric
tramways.

The second attempt to tunnel under the Severn gave South
Wales a short cut to London, and Britain the longest underwater
tunnel in the world, a record only recently broken by the
Japanese. The contractor who carried out the work, at the special
request of Sir John Hawkshaw the engineer, was Thomas
Walker, who had started his own business in partnership with
his brother Charles in 1871. Before that he had attended London
University, a rare distinction for a Victorian contractor, and had
spent two years with Brassey's company in Canada, settling there
for a further seven years, making railways in Lower Canada, now
known as Quebec. Work in Russia, Egypt and Sudan followed
before he settled in London to manage the construction of the
Metropolitan and the Metropolitan District lines from Edgware
Road to Mansion House. Work on the East London Railway
extension and dock work with Hawkshaw in the 1870s gave him
the reputation and experience that led Hawkshaw to insist that
he be the contractor for the Severn Tunnel, certainly the most
difficult single contract let up to that date. It is also one of the
best-documented contracts on record, since Thomas Walker
wrote a book about the construction of the tunnel and its
difficulties. Usually it was the engineer who wrote either a book
or gave a lecture on the subject to a learned society, but Walker
was no ordinary contractor. Sir John Hawkshaw it was who
wrote the preface to Walker's book.

Work had originally started on the tunnel in 1877, but the

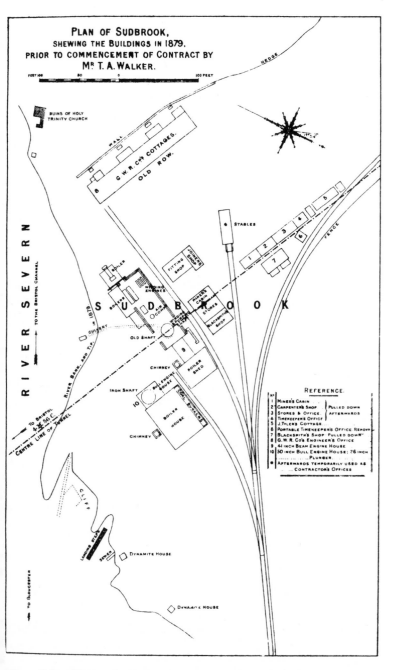

Plan of the village at Sudbrook, created to service construction work on the Severn Tunnel

inrush of water from the springs in the fractured rock flooded the works before even the headings from either bank met. The resumption of work under Hawkshaw, concurrently commencing the abortive Channel Tunnel in Kent, was a planned operation requiring the very best contracting work. It was a lengthy project, so a complete village and works was constructed at Sudbrook on the Welsh bank. The quality of the cottages, the hospital and the social facilities were superior to any seen on other contracts, as much because it was carried out from one site as the fact that Hawkshaw knew of 'no contractor who has displayed so much care and solicitude for the comfort and welfare of the workpeople employed by him'. The coffee taverns, nurses and mission halls were all part of the services to navvies and miners that were unusual at the time.

On this system three sets of men worked in each twenty-four hours, changing shifts at six in the morning, two in the afternoon and ten at night. Each shift was allowed half an hour in the middle of the shift for a hasty meal.

> I had insisted on the men working ten-hour shifts, and, during the shift, coming twice to bank for their meals.
>
> All the work having to be done by blasting, it was dangerous for the men to return to the faces immediately after the shots had been fired, because at that time dynamite was used, the fumes of which are dangerous.
>
> On the ten-hours system it was arranged that nearly all the blasting was done just before the men came out of the tunnel to their meals. The air was then clear by the time they went down again. The men commenced to work at six o'clock, and worked three hours. From nine to ten they came out of the tunnel, and had breakfast; going down again at ten, they worked till one o'clock; from one to two they came out to dinner, and from two till six they worked again to complete the ten-hour shift.[2]

Not all the changes inaugurated by Walker were appreciated by the men who had stayed at Sudbrook during the break caused by the inrush of the Great Spring:

> When the Great Spring broke in and drowned the tunnel in October 1879, the distance from the shaft to the face of the heading under the river was 10,100 feet, or more than a mile and three-quarters. All the skips were brought out by men pushing them that distance, the men

being known as 'runners out.' These 'runners out' had very short lengths to push the skips, and the cost, when the Company was working the heading, was more than ten times what it could have been done for by ponies, or perhaps twenty times that by proper hauling-engines.[3]

Although Walker was a good employer by the standards of the time, he was also a firm one when he saw his own interests threatened. His method of dealing with them had its desired effect:

There had been a bad spirit among the men from the time I had taken possession of the works. I believe they had wished that I should fail in pumping the water out of the tunnel. I am not quite sure that they had not wilfully caused some of the difficulties that had occurred; and now that the works were opened throughout, and there was a prospect of making better progress, they determined to make a stand, and either force me to abandon the work altogether, or to yield to their demands. This discontent first showed itself by their jeering at the men who took their meals with them up the long heading, asking them why they did not get tin hats made to carry their dinners in; and then by assaulting in the darkness, or when they could meet with them alone, men I had brought from a tunnel I had just finished at Dover.

At last on Saturday the 21st May, a notice appeared, written in chalk, at the top of the main shaft: 'I hope the _____ bond will break, and kill any man that goes down to work.'

The men gathered round the pit, but refused to go below.

It was Saturday morning, and the pay of the night-gangs would commence between eleven and twelve o'clock.

I may as well state here that on Saturday the men only worked seven hours, but were paid for ten. They went down, as on other days, at six; came up to breakfast from nine to ten, and the first, or day-shift, finished at two. The second, or night-shift, commencing at two, worked only till ten, making seven hours, with one off for a meal; and the works, except the pumping, were not carried on at all from 10 p.m. on Saturday till 6 a.m. on Monday.

After refusing to commence the shift they went off to the nearest public house, came back primed with drink; and gathered in front of the pay-office grumbling; but they never came to me or the foreman and stated any grievance or asked for any concession. They simply determined to make trouble and stop the works if they could. I was in the office at the time, so I went down into the middle of them, and said:

'Now what do you fellows want?'

No answer.

'Now tell me what you want, and don't stop hanging about here.'
Then one of them said:

'We want the eight-hour shifts'.

I said: 'My good men, you will never get that, if you stop here for a hundred years. There is a train at two o'clock, and if you don't make haste and get your money you will lose your train. You had better get your money as soon as you can, and go.'

The men looked very sheepish, went to the pay-office and got their money, and the works were absolutely deserted for the following four days.

This strike, as I have said, occurred on Saturday, and the next night (Sunday) the great timber pier at the Black Rock, where the ferry steamers landed their passengers, was burnt down, and there were not wanting people to say that it had been burnt by the men on strike; but, in my judgement, they were innocent of this. There had been a long period of dry weather, the timber in the pier was very old, and, above the level of high water, very dry; and I think some pleasure-seeker on Sunday had probably thrown away a fusee after lighting his pipe, and there being a high wind at the time, the fire had spread quickly. It probably arose either from this or from the careless raking out of the fire from the boiler of the engine which was used in lifting the luggage of passengers from the steamer at the end of the pier.

It was a good thing for the works that this strike occurred when it did, for it cleared away a number of bad characters who had gathered on the works; and from this time to the completion of the contract there was hardly any trouble with the men, and I think there was a thoroughly good feeling between employer and employed.[4]

The tunnelling experience that Walker had obtained in London was invaluable when he came to solve the problems of the weak and porous rocks under the Severn. Rock variations and water constantly slowed progress, making the work underground extremely unpleasant:

Before mining to place a head-tree, or a crown-bar, polling-boards must be driven by mauls as piles; and where the ground is wet, this is one of the most difficult operations miners have to perform, for the dirty water streams over the end of the piles, and at every blow of the maul is spattered on all the men that are near.

A considerable length of the Severn Tunnel, on the Gloucestershire side, was in loose gravel, full of water, and required this operation.

In the same ground the crown-bars had to be placed entirely outside the tunnel, and the brick-work of the arch completed under them, the space between the crown-bars being filled up to the polling-boards with rough brickwork or rubble.

In shaft-sinking, I have known cases, more than thirty years ago, where, when a depth say 20 or 30 feet, had been sunk from the top, a curb was placed, carried by iron rods, and in some cases by chains from timbers laid across the top of the shaft, and the brickwork for lining the shaft was built upon this curb; and in some cases the brickwork has been built continuously on the top of the shaft, and the lining lowered away till it reached the required level. In other cases short lengths have been taken out in the sinking, and the brickwork added below the first curb on other curbs placed from time to time.[5]

Thomas Walker took great pains to avoid accidents, but was philosophical enough to realise that on a work of this kind some were unavoidable. One such had a geological origin when, having advanced the face through treacherous coal shale,

the face slipped out off a concealed bed of rock, which stood at an angle of about 45 degrees, and in slipping knocked out the whole of the props under the sills. The knocking out of these props caused the sills to break; the upper part of the face then also slipped in, and we 'lost the length'. This was the only length we lost in the whole tunnel; and as the total number of lengths taken out was over 1,500, it shows that great care was exercised by the foremen and the miners, to be able to say that only one length of the 1,500 was lost.[6]

The losing of a length in such ground was, however, a serious matter, as the following instance shows:

It was under the river, but fortunately there were the hard beds of Pennant and conglomerate above the coal-shale, so that we had no reason to fear that the water would break into us.

As quickly as possible the top was secured, and then one of the most difficult operations in mining was commenced, viz., to pole through the broken ground.[7]

The most feared event in underwater tunnelling was an inrush of water from the river above. Should that happen, then the workers can only run uphill, hoping that the inrush will not overtake them. If the water came from a spring in the rock, then there was more hope of taming it before the whole works were flooded, and there was a repeat of the 1879 disaster in 1883, the worst such event happening while Walker was in charge.

As it had a drop there of more than 40 feet, the roar of the water, when you were in the tunnel was deafening. My first action on reaching the bottom of the shaft was to taste the water. To my great relief I found that it was fresh, and we, therefore, had no reason to suppose that we should not be able to contend with this difficulty, as we had with so many before.

It was evident, however, that the water was coming in at a rate very much exceeding our power to pump it out, and therefore the time that would elapse before it rose through the lower workings must be spent in precautionary measures. It was impossible to approach the head-wall in the lower heading, and the door there was open; but the men went up to see that the door in the upper heading was properly closed, and to put additional timbers in the sloping heading to secure the head-wall there.

As there was a hole existing from the tunnel at Sudbrook to the new pumping shaft on the south side of the line, bricklayers were at once started to close this hole with brickwork in cement. As soon as these works were started, I ascertained the following facts with regard to the inburst of the water.

The night-gang, working in the bottom heading westwards, had gone to work shortly after six o'clock, taking up skips with them, and had begun to shovel up the loose rock dislodged by the blasting, when the ganger said:

'There is more water here than usual – the "Grip" (a small ditch at the side of the heading) must be blocked. Push back a skip or two to clear it out.'

The men had hardly done so, when, to use the words of the ganger, 'the water broke in from the bottom of the face of the heading, rolling up all at once like a great horse'. It swept the men and the iron skips like so many chips out through the door and into the finished tunnel; and it was only when the water spread itself over the whole width of the tunnel that they were able to gather themselves up, and save themselves from being precipitated down the old shaft into the lower works. They were swept through the door without the power to check their passage, but they at once endeavoured to work their way back again up the heading, holding one another and clinging to the timbers at the side, to shut the door, if it were in any way possible. All their efforts failed, for the water was running down the heading in a stream ten feet wide and three feet six inches deep, and with such rapidity and force that no man could stand against it.

Anxiously we watched the rising of the water. We found that it was rapidly gaining upon the pumps; that it was already 10 or 12 feet deep in the tunnel under the shoots; that the men had all escaped; but that the horsekeeper had, in his terror, ridden off on one of the cobs, and left three others to drown.[8]

Despite the drama of the occasion, little permanent damage was done, Walker managing to continue excavations once the pumps had brought the water level down again. Work then continued steadily and uneventfully, apart from pumps breaking down and men getting hurt, until the Big Spring was finally conquered, allowing the completion of brickwork and a start to be made on tracklaying and finishing. The draining of the Big Spring was accomplished in 1885–6.

Sir John Hawkshaw then determined that it was necessary to provide pumping-plant to pump the whole of the water from the spring, and not to subject the brickwork of the tunnel to the enormous pressure it would have to sustain to exclude this water:

Arrangements were made with me to sink a large shaft at the side of the tunnel, 29 feet in internal diameter. In this shaft were to be fixed six large pumps with six 70-inch Cornish beam-engines fixed in a house which entirely covered the shaft. It was also determined to fix two 65-inch engines with two new pumps in the pumping-shaft at 5 miles 4 chains, and two 41-inch beam-engines with 29-inch pumps in the shaft at Sea-Wall.

A Guibal Fan, 40 feet in diameter and 12 feet wide, was ordered by the Company, and the designs made for the necessary buildings, comprising fanhouse, engine-house and boiler-house. Two Lancashire boilers, each 26 feet in length by 7 feet in diameter were provided for the fan, and a space provided for a third boiler, which was afterwards added. Twelve Lancashire boilers 28 feet in length and 7 feet in diameter, were provided for the pumping engines at Sudbrook, and a new engine and boiler-house were built at 5 miles 4 chains, in which four Cornish boilers already there belonging to the Company were fixed with three new Lancashire boilers.

The 29ft shaft, which was 35 feet in external diameter outside the brickwork, the circular wall being 3 feet in thickness, was sunk in the manner described in the account of the sinking of the other shafts, and without any difficulty from water, as a bore-hole was dropped down into the side-heading below.

The shaft was commenced the 8th February, 1886, and completed to the bottom on the 7th April. The brickwork lining of the shaft was completed on the 3rd June. The building of the engine-house at the top of the shaft was commenced on the 9th February, and completed on July 8th, 1886. The engines in this case were not only constructed, but were erected by Messrs. Harvey & Co. of Hayle, the pumps being fixed by me; and the first engine and pump were ready to start and were started on the 1st July 1886.

The length of the 12-inch cast-iron pipe laid in the side-heading was 515 feet; and when this pipe was running full bore, it still required a head of 70 feet to force the whole of the water through the length of pipe.[9]

The other hazards to the completion of the Severn Tunnel were epidemics and illness generally amongst the men. Had an epidemic been prolonged on either side of the Severn during construction, the works could have been brought to a halt, so as early as 1881 a 'fever hospital' had been set up on the Gloucestershire side of the river to eliminate typhoid. Improvements to the drinking-water supply had been the key to permanent elimination of that disease. Smallpox threatened to break out in Sudbrook after an epidemic had started in nearby Chepstow, so a second and more permanent 'fever hospital' was constructed in addition to the cottage hospital which had been completed in 1882:

> This hospital was completed and opened in the second week in October. A plan showing the arrangement of the wards and the dwelling house is given.
>
> Considering the magnitude of the undertaking, the difficulties encountered and the number of men employed night and day, we were very free from accidents during the six years the works were in progress; but still we found the hospital of the greatest value in treating both accidents and diseases, such as congestion of the lungs, rheumatic fever, etc. The principal illness that the men suffered from was pneumonia, caused no doubt by the great heat and damp below, and then careless exposure when they came out of the works.
>
> Besides the general wards in the hospital, we had an operating-room, an emergency-ward, and a ward for women and children.[10]

Nearly 4,000 men were employed on the scheme at its peak, slightly more than half of them on the Monmouthshire bank. John Price in Gloucestershire and Joseph Talbot on the Monmouthshire side were the trusted principal foremen who enabled Walker to fulfil other contracts simultaneously. In 1884 he had undertaken work on the nearby Barry Dock & Railways for David Davies, then one of the greatest coalowners in South Wales. The work continued for five years, employing another 2,000 men. At the opening on 18 July 1889, he presided at a dinner given to his navvies who had not been invited to the main celebration, which Walker missed.

Two such operations overlapping each other should have been enough for any man, but Thomas Walker took on two more enormous works, the Manchester Ship Canal, which contract he had wrested from Lucas & Aird and Buenos Aires harbour in Argentina. The Manchester Ship Canal was by far the largest of these contracts, employing 14,000 men, 171 locomotives and 90 excavating machines, working round the clock. The Buenos Aires undertaking employed a further 5,000 men. Since Walker was operating without partners, his personal achievement seems that much greater for a man working on three of the greatest projects of the period at the age of sixty. He contracted Bright's disease, of which he died on 25 October 1889, the Barry project completed as far as he was concerned, but the other two works were left to others. The Manchester Ship Canal was eventually completed in 1894 by Sir John Jackson. Sir John Hawkshaw summed up the man and the immensity of the tasks he undertook and which became too much even for him:

> In my long experience of contractors, extending over more than fifty years, I have never met with anyone surpassing Mr Walker for despatch in carrying out works. This arose not only from his great anxiety always to fulfil his engagements, but also from the very great interest he took in all the constructive details of his work. This led him to disregard considerations of expense when difficulties were met with which had to be overcome. If more plant was required it was procured at once, if more temporary work was necessary it was ordered to be done forthwith; and so questions of loss or gain to himself never caused delay. Moreover, taking such interest as he did in his works, it followed that none but the best class of work would satisfy him.
>
> Mr Walker's practice of going into all the details of his works himself brought upon him an immense amount of labour over and above that which must necessarily fall to the lot of a large contractor, and it probably tended to shorten his life. When the works he had in hand were of smaller magnitude the course he pursued was practicable; but when, as at the close of his life, they had become of great extent and importance it ceased to be possible for one brain to deal with all the details arising from them.[11]

Arrol, Waddell and Walker proved that bridging and tunnelling could be taken much further than hitherto where water was concerned. Longer tunnels and bridges had already been built on the continent and in the USA, but the spans of the bridges or the length of tunnel under water did not compare with the British achievements. The network of tube lines in London carried the expertise gained in the 1880s a stage further, thus ending the era of innovation and increasingly complex contracts that made the period from 1880 to World War I one of outstanding interest. The latter-day contractor was often inventive – for instance J. W. Willans solved the problems of erecting the Liverpool Overhead Railway in 1894 by designing a steel-erecting machine of his own which, after practice, put up 650ft of completed steel spans a week.

As railway building came to an end in the first decade of the twentieth century, so contractors specialising in railway work tended to die out; Sir Thomas Firbank was probably the last to describe himself purely as a railway contractor. Firms which built the later railways both at home and overseas, like Monk & Newall, Topham, Jones & Railton, Logan & Hemingway and Thomas Oliver seem to have regarded themselves as general contractors with no special commitment to railways. The engineering, design and management sides of the later firms were much larger than those of the Victorian railway contractors. No longer did the man at the top have to rely on his brain crammed with detail. The organisation was often better than the individual, although there were still some very colourful figures who dominated their companies, like the McAlpines. No longer was it possible to scribble an estimate on the back of an envelope as had David Davies, or work largely by word of mouth like Brassey.

Few railway contractors even before 1866 spent their whole lives making railways. The committed Firbanks built residential property, albeit for the Manchester, Sheffield & Lincolnshire Railway and the South Eastern Railway. The financial, constructional and management skills that they had acquired were applicable to a wide range of other work, in which most of the larger contractors indulged at one time or another.

David Davies, for instance, gave up railway contracting after successful completion of the Manchester & Milford Railway, apart from the little Van Railway which he built in 1871. At the end of the M&MR contract, he and his partner, Frederick Beeston junior, gave a dinner to their workmen in Aberystwyth at the Belle Vue Hotel where the men presented Davies with a valuable clock. Davies responded with one of his lengthy but humorous speeches, saying that he was leaving railway contracting just when they were ready to do justice to greater contracts, but he did not want to build the M&MR extension to Llanidloes, abandoned by his partner's father, as he abhorred work which would leave him and his men jobless. Rather he had already taken a lease on coal rights in the Rhondda Valley from Crawshay Bailey in 1864, gradually building up to a single large area of 8,000 acres. He sank his first shaft at Cwmparc in January 1865, although after more than a year's work, the miners had still not reached the coal seams hoped for, and Davies' resources, still involved with two uncompleted railways, were stretched to the limit. He called a meeting of the miners and told them frankly that whilst he was sure that they were near to coal, he could not go on. He admitted that he was down to his last half-crown, which a cheeky miner said they would take, so it was tossed to him as Davies stalked out. The effect of this was an impromptu meeting at which it was decided that the men would work for a week without wages, enough to reach the upper steam coal seam, the foundation of Davies' coal-mining fortune. By 1870 Davies had three collieries at work producing nearly 350,000 tons a year, and his Ocean Collieries Group was the second most productive in the South Wales coalfield. In the next twenty years, collieries were developed in other parts of the coalfield, eventually bringing production to 1¾m tons a year by 1890 and employing over 5,000 men, part of the vast export trade that South Wales developed with its steam, gas and anthracite coals.

Railway management was also a field that concerned David Davies from the time he had leased the little local railway he first built. From 1868 until 1879 he was a director of the Cambrian Railways, resigning over the run-down condition into which the line got, with consequent risk to life and limb. The receivership into which the CR fell five years later was a result of the over-capitalisation and general neglect that Davies sought to avoid by drastic changes in 1879. He also became a director of the Taff Vale Railway in 1870, of which line he was a major customer, and the Brecon & Merthyr Railway, which had extended towards Newport and became a modestly important coal railway. For a year he was even on the board of the stately LNWR, whose Vale of Clwyd subsidiary he had built in his early days. His coal exporting led to overseas links and directorships of a Spanish and a Brazilian railway.

The Barry Dock & Railways arose out of Davies' dissatisfaction with the service he got from the TVR and the Bute Dock in Cardiff, together originally responsible for shipping most of his coal. The glut of traffic slowly filtering down the Rhondda and Taff valleys often came to a standstill, resulting in expensive delays for the colliery-owned wagons. The concept of the Barry Dock & Railways (the Barry Railway from 1891) was to bypass Cardiff and create a new port which would tap the existing coal-mines. After a titanic battle in parliament, lasting some four years, the Act was granted on 14 August 1884, with the contract let only a few weeks later to Thomas Walker.

Parliament has always seemed attractive to contractors, most of whom could already work at several jobs simultaneously. Although narrowly defeated in the 1865 election at Cardigan, David Davies was returned for that constituency in 1874 when the sitting Liberal stepped down after disagreement with the local party. As a former working man who had made himself into a great capitalist, he was something of a labour expert in an aristocratic and bourgeois House of Commons. His other hobby-horse was temperance, railing at the waste in time and accidents resulting from drink. He fell out with the Liberal Party over Home Rule, becoming a Liberal Unionist, and eventually lost his seat by a mere nine votes to a Gladstonian Liberal in 1886. His death four years later ended one of the greatest careers undertaken almost solely in Wales, apart from his parliamentary activities, which were largely on behalf of a very Welsh constituency.

Charles Lucas and Sir John Kelk between them succeeded Cubitt and Peto as the main builders of public and private buildings in Victorian London. Cubitt and Peto moved into railway contracting after very successful careers which involved constructing much of Belgravia, Cubitt Town, the great London clubs in Pall Mall, Nelson's Column and the Houses of Parliament. With such contractors, it is not surprising that architects and engineers could confidently design such bold edifices as Euston, Shrewsbury Station and the tunnels and viaducts whose massive decoration sometimes triumphed over their functionalism. Charles Lucas started his working life under Peto, then branched out to build the resort side of Lowestoft, the Esplanade and Marine Parade, its largest hotels and a new church at Kirkley Cliff. Moving to London, he continued hotel building with the station hotels at London Bridge, Cannon Street and Charing Cross, and the Langham Hotel, now part of the BBC complex, opposite Broadcasting House. In the 1860s, while his railway business was growing, he did not neglect his other building works; indeed these grew more impressive as he was partnered by Kelk, who had been apprenticed to Thomas Cubitt, thus providing continuity in the breath-taking expansion of Victorian London. This link with Lucas Brothers started in 1860 and resulted not only in the building of much of the steam-hauled underground system, but in the private and public buildings that it served. The London exhibition of 1862 was a joint enterprise, loss-making, but hardly ruinous when so much profit was being made by them in new housing development. As railway contractors they had early warning of where profitable sites would be located. The Royal Albert Hall and much of the Covent Garden complex were probably the peaks of Lucas's career, whilst Victoria Station was regarded by Kelk as his *magnum opus*. Their distinctive mid-nineteenth-century style of building can best be traced in London by riding around the Inner Circle (Circle Line) which they largely built, alighting especially at Liverpool Street, South Kensington, Victoria and Embankment, where the largest concentrations of their structures are to be found, some of the soundest in London more than a century old. Even the architectural style is now being talked of more appreciatively after decades of being despised.

Sir Charles Fox was one of the rare breed of engineer-contractors who seemed to be able to carry out both functions without too many hitches. He trained as a surgeon before joining the Liverpool & Manchester Railway, serving as a fireman and learning all that was to be learned of railways, inventing, building, testing and experimenting until he set up in practice himself. His work in erecting the Crystal Palace earned him a knighthood, his work in removing it to Sydenham much profit and railway contracts.

The Great Exhibition of 1851 is an interesting example of the interaction between railway contracting and other projects. The Crystal Palace Committee had William Cubitt as a prominent member. The designer, Sir Joseph Paxton, later became a director of the West End & Crystal Palace Railway. His design was accepted after the rejection of designs by Isambard Kingdom Brunel amongst others.

Delays in deciding which design was the most suitable meant that Paxton's plans were accepted as late as July 1850, the Hyde Park site becoming available at the end of the month, a mere ten months from the planned opening date. Right through July and August 1850 Fox toiled for eighteen hours a day at his London office in Spring Gardens preparing the working drawings. His partner, Henderson, took the drawings 'hot from the board' and translated them into reality, using some of the products of Fox, Henderson & Co, engineers and ironmasters of Smethwick, half the sheet glass output of the country, miles of gas piping and much else. The building was completely glazed by January 1851 with the help of an ingenious glazing trolley designed by the firm and all was ready for the spring opening. The cavernous interior was a model for the future train sheds which became such a feature of railway stations in the second half of the nineteenth century.

Sir Charles Fox was joined by his sons Douglas and Francis in forming one of the greatest engineering teams in the second half of the nineteenth century, still with us today as Freeman, Fox & Partners. The railway contracting side of Fox's interests, Fox, Henderson & Co, not only contracted worldwide, but manufactured wheels and other types of railway plant, made road bridges and pioneered narrow gauge railways.

As railway contracting waned in the late nineteenth century, so the railway content of contractors' work also declined. Weetman Pearson made the greatest part of his fortune in prospecting for and finding oil in Mexico, where his firm, Mexican Eagle, was in direct competition to the American giants. Public utility work also became a very important part of his contracting services. Indeed public utilities such as waterworks, sewage tunnels and treatment works, gas and later electricity undertakings became one of Britain's great export industries. The skills of tunnelling across London to make the main sewers had been acquired while building canals and then railways, and could be applied by Brassey when he built the northern tunnel of London's sewage system. John Aird's main contributions were in the field of gas and water provision, culminating in the massive Beckton gasworks on the Thames. The construction of docks likewise involved most of the major contractors, the excavation, masonry work and dockside structures having similar requirements to those of railway building, with the added advantage that they were usually carried out on the fringe of urban areas, thus making labour and its needs much less of a problem.

The emergence of railway contractors as an identifiable group of businessmen in the late 1830s started off a chain of events that changed the whole nature of the world in the next eighty years. The skills that they acquired in Staffordshire and Norfolk, Montgomeryshire and Lancashire, for example, were released worldwide in a remarkably short space of time, most of the mistakes having been ironed out by trial and error in Britain. Complete working systems and trained operatives could be sent abroad as part of a package deal. Methods of finance were conceived, if not perfected, that enabled poor districts and poor countries to bring in a railway and pay for it later, once the agriculture, mines or forests were being exploited. The rails, locomotives, wagons, skilled labour and much of the capital came from Britain and repaid Britain for decades thereafter. It could have been done in other ways, but without the titanic energies of the handful of major contractors, the process would have occurred slower and later. They had many faults, but often these were exaggerated by their working within the system which they found. Brassey preferred a planned system of state railways, as it avoided the wasteful competition that he saw too much of in the 1860s. David Davies and Weetman Pearson actively worked in Parliament to better the lot of the working man and openly declared against faults in the system as they saw it. What seems to be almost certain is that they did their work better and treated their workmen in a more satisfactory manner than the conglomeration of small contractors who had started the railway building era.

9
The Minor League

Although so much of the construction of our railways was under-taken by substantial contractors, there were many smaller firms which operated in the field with varying success. In the early years large numbers of small contracting firms were employed. When they had differences with the railway company, recourse to the law was often slow and unproductive, as the case of Macintosh v GWR shows. The original dispute with Brunel began before 1840 and was not finished until after David Macintosh's death:

It cannot be otherwise than satisfactory to this great proprietary to learn that the long-pending and consequently expensive suit instituted in 1847 by the celebrated contractor, Mr Macintosh was at length arranged. The sum claimed from the Great Western went to the enormous length of £248,000. It may be remembered that the answers of the company, in the earlier stages of the suit, were felt to be so complete that the plaintiff lay back for several years; and that in 1852, when the company applied for dismissal of the inquiry for want of prosecution a revival of the litigation took place. Nothing further, however, appears to have been attempted for a period of two years, when a number of affidavits were filed, and at length in April 1855, the cause came on for hearing before Vice-Chancellor Stuart, who made a decree directing the chief clerk to inquire what was due to the plaintiff under the various contracts. In January 1856 Mr Macintosh died, and the suit was revived by his personal representative. Considerable time was necessarily occupied in taking the accounts, but ultimately the chief clerk made his certificate, to which the company took a number of exceptions, and these came on for hearing in January 1865, when the Vice-Chancellor made an order enjoining the company to pay the sum of £148,000 with interest at the rate of 4 per cent from February 1864 as well as the costs of the suit. The Great Western appealed against this decision, and the case has since been brought up for argument before the Lord Chancellor on several occasions. The claims of the company, as set off against the contractor, having been admitted to a great extent, and the original claim of £248,000 having been reduced by Vice-Chancellor Stuart to £148,000, the chief points of the remaining contest related to payment of interest and costs of the suit, the company naturally contending that as a debt was at all times acknowledged and that as they were prepared on every occasion to ascertain its exact amount, the decision in regard to liability for interest and costs ought to be reversed. This solution of the difficulty, we are glad to learn has at length been obtained, the plaintiff having consented to accept a less sum than that awarded by the Vice-Chancellor (viz. £120,000) in full of all demands. In closing this dreary yet eventless history, we are satisfied that its termination will prove satisfactory to the proprietors.[1]

The larger companies tried to avoid the smaller contractors with their inexperienced work-forces, once both major railways and major contractors had become established. Smaller local railways were not in such a happy position, usually being unable to find ready cash for payment to a prominent contractor like Joseph Firbank. The merchants, landed gentry and farmers who made up the boards of such companies sometimes came to grief when dealing with contractors in difficult circumstances:

Within the last few days the works of the Mistley Thorpe and Walton Railway in the parish of Bradfield and about one mile south of the town of Manningtree, have been the scene of a 'battle'. The casus belli may be briefly stated. There had been some discontent on the part of the company and their engineer, Mr Cooke, at the works not being carried on more rapidly by the contractor, Mr Munro; and the relations between the parties having become embittered from this circumstance, it was deemed advisable to separate, and the results of the negotiations was that Mr Monro, [sic] with the full concurrence of the Board of Directors, assigned the completion of his contract to another contractor, Mr Furness. After this assignment had been made, however, an objection was raised by Mr Furness to take from Mr Munro a quantity of rails and other material, which the latter considered a part of the arrangement; and, secondly, the company's engineer in scrutinizing a 'little bill' of £2,000 sent in by Mr Munro, suggested that there was an 0 too many, and proposed to tax off the something more than trifling amount of £1,800. Under these circumstances Mr Munro refused to give up possession of the works; and on the other hand Mr Furness, the new contractor, called upon the company to give him the necessary induction to his undertaking. After some unsuccessful parleying it became evident that force alone could effect a dislodgement, and the 11th of April was chosen for the fight.

The late contractor's force consisted of some 50 navvies under the command of his agent, veteran 'General' Fryer, who lately fought so fierce and stern a campaign with a certain Highway Board not a hundred miles from Lavenham; and although the Board remained nominally masters of the field, he at least succeeded in dictating his own terms, as well as his own time of surrender. On the part of the company some 60 lumpers or long-shore men had been brought up from Harwich, the command of whom was taken by Engineer-General Cooke, assisted by the Solicitors-General Cobbold and Owen and Secretary General Size. General Fryer, in order not to be taken in the rear, chose [sic] the head of a cutting as his position of defence, and with equal determination, though in less polished phrase, hurled Fitz James's defence at the approaching foe –

> 'Come one, come all, this rock shall fly
> From its firm base as soon as I.'

The position was a somewhat difficult one to turn, and several smart skirmishes were engaged in without any decisive result. At length, however, the company's force, responding to General Cooke's appeal to their gallantry, 'Lumpers, up and at 'em,' made a rush and captured General Fryer, while the navvies, with equal determination and apparently equal strength seized him from behind.

> 'Now Gallant Saxon, hold thine own,
> No maiden's arms are round thee thrown;
> That grasp of might thou well could'st feel,
> Through bars of brass or triple steel;'

And truly the luckless general seemed in imminent peril either of strangulation or dismemberment. Eventually the lumpers prevailed over the navvies, who fled in disorder, leaving their General to be 'lifted' ignominiously beyond the Company's boundaries. Fryer, however, was not the man to succumb to a first reverse; collecting the scattered remnants of his force he marched to the next cutting, and there made a second stand, but his navvies were evidently indisposed to come again to close quarters with the sturdy lumpers; and although General himself disdained to fly he could only offer a passive resistance, and the process of 'lifting' was again performed upon his person. Still undismayed, he attempted a third stand at another point of the line; but further resistance was evidently useless, and having been once more ousted, the new contractor was installed in possession of the works without more opposition on the part of his predecessor, and the questions at issue between them as well as between Mr Munro and the Company, were left to be determined by another tribunal.

Thus ended the 'Battle of Bradfield' – happily without bloodshed;

and although hard words and occasionally hard blows were not
wanting, the contest on the whole was carried out with all the
courtesies of modern and civilised warfare.[2]

The Stephensons employed sub-contractors and later contractors who took over relatively small sections of lines to be
built, tunnels to be excavated or viaducts to be erected, all under
their direction; such single contracts rarely exceeded £100,000.
When contractors failed, as at Kilsby, the company engineer had
to supervise the works directly. The task was not very popular
with engineers who, despite the distaste that many had for contractors, realised that contractors could handle navvies and
craftsmen far better than they themselves usually could. It was
with some reluctance that the Midland Railway took over No 1
contract on the Settle and Carlisle line from Ashwell. There was
less reluctance in Norfolk in the 1870s and 1880s, when a
number of poverty stricken local railways in that county either
became so frustrated with contractors or thought that they could
undercut them, that there was a veritable outbreak of do-it-
yourself railway building, using local craftsmen and railway
workers as well as outside labour under company control.

The little Thetford & Watton Railway, for example, obtained
an Act to build a short branch line from Roudham Junction on
the Great Eastern's Ely to Norwich line on 12 July 1866. Its aims
were modest, its capital of £45,000 was subscribed to the extent
of £14,350 within two months of the Act, so tenders for the
contract were sought in May 1867, receiving three replies.
William Smith Simpson quoted £15,200, T. Greenhill some
£14,250, while an amazingly low £9,907 came from Richard
Walker of Felixstowe. The reason for the very low quotation
came in the next week by letter (original spelling adhered to):

21-5-67   From: R. Walker, Felixstowe.
Dear Sir,

   In going over the estimate for the above line I was veary sorrow to
find my Clark had made a great mistake having left out the whole of
the earthwork. Consequently I must decline to take the contract at
the sum mentioned but will send you an amended tender which I
Hope the Directors will accept and allso se how the mestake was
made,

                              Yours truly,
                              Ric'd Walker.

The new estimate of £13,243, £2,000 of it acceptable in debentures, was still lower than that of the others, so was accepted. The low additional amount for the earthworks indicates the easy nature of building on this flat, waterless plateau.

At first Walker progressed rapidly enough for Great Eastern supervision to be dispensed with, leaving local directors in charge. Completion by 1 July 1868 was expected, so tenders for four clay-lump cottages at £640 were put out and another at a level crossing for £118 10s 0d, low even for Victorian Norfolk. The stations were more substantial. Mr Forest quoted £331 for the black flint station houses at Stow Bedon and Wretham. He also took the contracts for the goods and engine sheds at Watton.

Richard Walker missed his deadline, however, and the Great Eastern demanded that a £2,000 station be built at Roudham Junction to deliver all traffic there. The local directors refused and went to a railway equipment contractor, a Mr Barton, who was willing to supply turntable, telegraph and junction for debentures, as well as a locomotive and two carriages for £20 9s 6d per week. Such treachery did not please the Great Eastern and when Mr Barton failed to fulfil his promises and the Board of Trade failed to pass Walker's work, the little railway was in difficulties. It managed to open the line without a junction on 26 January 1869, later obtaining a pair of Manning Wardle tank engines, which worked the little branch line economically. This modest success went to the heads of the local directors, who promoted an extension Bill under the title of the Watton & Swaffham Railway, hoping to gain running powers northwards into King's Lynn and southwards to join the Bury & Thetford Railway, still being built. This would then provide a through route from Lynn to Bury. For this dubiously viable extension, £60,000 of new capital had to be raised, but only £2,995 was subscribed by September 1873, rising to £4,169 by the following March. Yet no less than £47,077 had been spent on construction, only made good by the massive issue of Lloyd's bonds. The contractor who accepted this method of finance was a Robert Birch, who had as site agent one John Cook. Cook's work was noted by the directors to be good, but Birch, though closely supervised, had a poor relationship with the directors, resulting in the ending of his contract in February 1874. Mutual litigation ensued to no avail. Meanwhile, John Cook was retained to supervise labour and sub-contractors. Richard Walker appeared as sub-contractor for earthworks, completing what Robert Birch had abandoned.

The Bury & Thetford line to the south found great difficulty in raising capital of £100,000, only some £7,508 being subscribed. Quarrels with the original contractor resulted in a policy of small contracts being let as money from bonds or loans was raised. The sub-contractors were only willing to work if their money was guaranteed. In this way, it took some ten years to produce a light, poorly constructed line which opened on 1 March 1876.

Meanwhile the Watton & Swaffham Railway was equipping itself for through traffic. Stone for ballast had to be brought from quarries at Whatstandwell in Derbyshire at 1s 8d per cubic yard. Girders came from Woodside Ironworks at Dudley in Worcestershire, Ransome & Rapier of Ipswich provided the level crossings and McKenzie & Holland of Worcester supplied the signalling equipment. Moules Patent Earth Closet at 12s 0d and half-a-dozen cane chairs at 4s 6d each provided creature comforts at Holme Hale, the only intermediate station. Every item was meticulously ordered and checked on arrival by company staff. During the course of delivery it was noted that a tallyman at Burt Boulton's timber yard had invoiced the same load twice, 'having made a mistake for which he has been discharged'. John Cook inspected and signed for each item, each painting job and every installation. At the peak of his work, he had 100 navvies to supervise. Cash for these payments came from the issue of Lloyd's bonds to Sir T. N. Abdy of Romford, with an interest rate of 6 per cent per year, some were made out to the engineer John Valentine and to Robert Birch for work done up to February 1874. In addition the Thetford & Watton Railway subscribed £10,000. In this welter of debt, the through route was eventually opened on 1 March 1876 using locomotives and stock owned by the T&WR against outright opposition from the GER, which refused water to the engines at Bury. The GER leased the three lines after they had staggered from one crisis to another for some three years, eventually liquidating the bonds in 1898 and buying £60,000 of the W&SR Ordinary stock for £6,062 10s 0d. Only John Cook seems to have come well out of the mess, because he was employed by the East Norfolk Railway to extend their line from North Walsham to Cromer in 1875, after Lucas Brothers had been refused the contract.

John Cook's appointment as company agent coincided with the issue of new shares by the East Norfolk Railway in July 1875. The line was supported by the GER but had several local directors on the board. Cook received £1,000 on account to buy plant, harness, provender for the horses, bricks and tools. Rails came from his W&SR work, where some were surplus to requirement. The local landowners, who were already substantial shareholders, readily made land available and permitted the removal of ballast and brickearth, and permitted brickyards to be set up *en route*. Labour was scarce because the harvest had started, added to which the earthworks were difficult, since much of the ground was boulder clay, stiff tenacious stuff with large rocks in it which blunted pickaxes when struck.

The cash flow to John Cook was slow. After nearly four months only £4,554 had been spent. Second-hand plant was obtained from the W&SR for £1,240, the works of Lucas Brothers south of North Walsham were scoured for materials, while the local brickworks were able to sell all that they could produce, but their quality was poor for structural work. A locomotive arrived in February 1876, but it was cut off from the existing line since the bridge at North Walsham had yet to be built. All materials had to be horse carted to the light tramways on site. The only mechanical contrivance was a steam-powered saw-bench, while with only 150 men at work, the date of completion given by the directors as August 1876 was totally unrealistic. Meanwhile, John Cook in his pony and trap was supervising work at six points, scouring the country for plant, horses and materials, as well as attending fortnightly meetings with the directors at Liverpool Street.

With the approach of summer 1876, a compromise was reached whereby Cook was urged to open the line to Gunton, the only intermediate station. He was authorised to purchase more of everything, twenty carthorses in Lambeth, horses, wagons and rails at Aberdare, and more wagons and plant from the Settle and Carlisle line. The new tempo allowed Gunton Station to be opened as a temporary terminal on 29 July 1876 whence the GER provided horse buses at rail fares to Cromer for what remained of the summer season.

The executive committee at last started to take the matter seriously, allowing Cook to employ up to 400 men by the late autumn. Where materials failed to arrive from suppliers, the GER provided them. Edward Wilson & Co, the engineers to the line, persuaded suppliers to reduce estimates for signals, and such items as turntables and rails were subject to a large number of tenders to get the lowest quotation. Although the line was officially opened on 26 March 1877, much remained to be done, Cook needing £7,123 to complete the line in April of that year. Money from the GER and Charles Parkes, the GER director, was needed to pay for this completion. It was thus with some relief that the ENR board turned to a good, reliable contracting firm, the Waddells, for their next line – the Aylsham Extension.

While the ENR was being built, a new series of lines was constructed across Norfolk by Messrs Wilkinson & Jarvis. They constructed the Midland & Great Northern Joint Railway which was a less than fortunate railway. Their approach and methods were reminiscent of an earlier period of tortuous financing and hand-to-mouth expediency, but they did provide a remote area with more railways than it really required and brought the Norfolk coast to the notice of holidaymakers who might not have been tempted to travel there, had only the Great Eastern routes been available.

Further little railways in the county were promoted by the same contractors-cum-civil engineers, the Great Yarmouth & Stalham (Light) Railway in the east and the Lynn & Fakenham Railway in the west. By circulating the local landowners and businessmen they had established the idea that, although these lines were to get their Bills through Parliament on the basis of being local lines connecting parts of Norfolk, unjustly neglected by the Great Eastern, they were eventually to be joined to form a major through route. Landowners were to receive shares for their land and were able, within reason, to choose the best route for the railway. Sir Edmund Lacon, MP for Yarmouth, banker and brewer extraordinary, promoted the line from his end; Sir William Browne ffolkes, MP, and the noble landowners along the way took care of the other end of the line. Eventually, by issuing shares at ever increasing discounts, drafting Lloyd's bonds and expending nearly £1,500,000 in capital and loans, they succeeded by 1883 in completing a route from King's Lynn to Yarmouth with a branch from Melton Constable to Norwich and a barely started branch to Blakeney, some eight years after they first entered the district. Their package-deal approach, from first sowing the idea in the minds of local landlords, then explaining that it would largely be made at little cost to them and at great advantage in reduced transport costs, was a classic of its kind. The shoestring financing left a poorly built line with huge debts that the likely traffic could not possibly support. Fittingly the line was linked westwards to the Waring Brothers' Midland & Eastern Railway, and the new manager brought in to run the Wilkinson & Jarvis lines was Robert Read, who had spent the previous two decades keeping the bailiffs at bay on the Somerset & Dorset Railway, a process which he repeated on the newly formed Eastern & Midlands Railway. It took another £1m in the 1890s, injected by the Midland and the Great Northern railways, to put the line to rights and make it reasonably profitable.

When they left Norfolk in mid-1883, the proposed Blakeney line was unfinished, terminating short of the first station, Holt. One of the contractor's staff, William Marriott, had stayed with the newly formed Eastern & Midlands Railway and been appointed engineer, so it fell to him to complete the line to Holt as quickly and cheaply as possible, in order to generate more desperately needed traffic. This was a successful exercise, resulting in two further lines being built by him with company labour and local sub-contractors – the Lynn Loop and the Cromer Undertaking.

The E&MR paid no dividends, ordinary or deferred, so in order to finance these lines the general manager of the line, Robert Read (also of the Somerset & Dorset Railway), obtained

sanction for the issue of £240,000 of Guaranteed 5 per cent
Preference Stock for the Cromer Undertaking and £100,000 for
the Lynn Loop. These stocks were separated from the main
capital and their interest was paid from receipts on these lines
rather than from general funds, of which there was a marked
absence. For four years they were actually paid, but succumbed
to the receivership into which the E&MR was plunged in 1889.

A bridge built near Cromer on the Norfolk & Suffolk Joint Railways in 1906

What the E&MR did achieve with Marriott's direction of the
new works, was lines made promptly and for approximately
£10,000 a mile, despite the heavy gradients out of Sheringham
and the massive earthworks around Holt. To lower the cost of
other installations, Marriott made many of the permanent way
necessities and the signalling equipment in the little company
works at Melton Constable.

As an experiment under difficult conditions, it was
undoubtedly a success with William Marriott in charge, but
when the system grew in the 1890s, his talents were needed
elsewhere, so for the building of the Mundesley branch and other

extensions, the services of conventional contractors were again used.

A final surge in local construction came in the two decades before World War I. The Light Railways Act of 1896 enabled promoters to obtain grants and loans from the Treasury and local authorities for the building of cheap rural railways. The remainder of the shares in such lines were taken up by local gentry, merchants and farmers.

John Strachan of Cardiff built the Welshpool & Llanfair Railway and the Tanat Valley Railway on the Welsh borders at the turn of the century. He used just over 100 men and a single locomotive, adequate for slow construction with relatively light earthworks. His waywardness in running a private goods and passenger service before the official opening of the TVR and working on the sabbath did little to endear him to the directors, but at least both lines were finished; the Mid-Suffolk Light Railway was only half finished when the chairman was bankrupted and the money for construction ran out. Two decades of receivership and a life of perpetual poverty followed for that unfortunate line.

After construction, a period of maintenance by contractors was normal, in order to adjust the road when embankments or cutting walls slipped during consolidation, and also to tidy up unfinished or poorly executed work. Meanwhile, outstanding matters between contractor and railway were discussed, and where unresolved, went to arbitration. Duncan Kennedy was finishing the work on the Ballachulish branch for a year after the opening on 24 August 1903. He had fifty labourers, six gangers to oversee them, a timekeeper and use of an old locomotive for the maintenance train. As the track bedded down, so the speed limit was raised, and the labourers who proved satisfactory and steady men were taken on as platelayers by the Caledonian Railway, thus forming a continuing link with the construction period for local workmen.

The contractor was usually a transient figure. A few who started in a small way later became great. In a few cases the sub-contractors of the late nineteenth century became the giants of the twentieth century – men such as Mowlem, McAlpine and

Wimpey. Charles Chambers of Westminster was something of an exception. He built the little Southwold Railway in 1878–9. A decade later he was involved in a forlorn attempt to reopen the Potteries Railway which later became the Shropshire & Montgomeryshire Light Railway. He was still active, in a small way, on the Golden Valley Railway in Herefordshire at the end of the century, where we find him haggling over terms for the GWR's takeover of that bankrupt concern. He eventually accepted £2,000 to discharge all his claims on a line for which he had originally accepted £104,000 in shares and debentures of various descriptions.

After World War I there were few openings in railway contracting for beginners. The growth areas by then were in house and road construction, a route to expansion which some of the present-day railway contractors used to grow in the inter-war period. An example of this was Frank Taylor, founder of Taylor Woodrow Ltd, who started by building a pair of houses in Blackpool in 1919. Estate construction in the 1930s and wartime government contracts took him into the big league, in which capacity he successfully tendered for the Euston Station rebuilding contract in the 1960s.

10

The Locomotive Fleets of the Great Contractors

In addition to the barrows, planks, spades and carts of the actual digging operations, contractors had their own temporary rail track and spoil wagons to take the rock and earth from where it was dug to where it was dumped. Early motive power was provided by men and horses, but as the size of operations grew and the length of journeys to the dumping points lengthened, so it became necessary to use locomotives. The primitive tracks and frequent derailments deterred the railway companies from loaning their own locomotives except in extreme circumstances, so second-hand engines were used at first and later specialised light tank engines were built to do the job, notably by Manning Wardle. These were small four- and six-coupled tank engines, well sprung and mechanically simple, a type of engine whose basic design was used for many decades from the middle of the nineteenth century.

The second type of locomotive fleet owned by the great contractors was of a type suited to running the railway when complete. Several early railways were built and operated by contractors such as Brassey and Peto, who also leased lines from the shareholders. The practice was seen as late as the 1880s when Messrs Wilkinson & Jarvis were operating the lines which later became the Eastern & Midlands Railway in Norfolk. In many cases the engines were later purchased by the railway company and became part of their permanent stock, but there were also cases of movement of engines between railways in which a contractor had interests (see Chapter 5) and also of trading in engines, many of which ended up in Boulton's Siding, near Manchester, while awaiting a new owner. This siding was a resting place for many and varied locomotives between periods of duty with contractors or industrial users. Sales, rentals and leases were all negotiated, as were trade-ins and repossessions.

Just how varied were the careers of some of the earlier contractors' locomotives is illustrated by the story of *Trent*, an 0-6-0ST which started life as one of the elegant little Sharp Stewart 2-2-2 express engines which graced the Great Northern Railway in its earlier years. The CME, Archibald Sturrock, converted some of these engines to 0-4-2s to give them greater adhesion on the steeply graded suburban lines. On retirement from this work, *Trent* was overhauled at Isaac Watt Boulton's Guide Bridge works near Manchester in 1865, and then hired out successively for contracting work at Dartford with James Rennie & Co. Following this John Aird & Co had her, and she was also used by John Morton to build the Central Wales Railway (later the LNWR line from Shrewsbury to Swansea) before being rebuilt as an 0-6-0ST in 1871, using many second-hand parts, eventually being sold two years later to an ironstone company in the Midlands.

Even a well-established contractor such as Brassey found it useful to use Boulton's services. His own design of geared locomotive, *Rattlesnake*, was used by Brassey to build the Runcorn Bridge in 1866, and the engine was sold back to

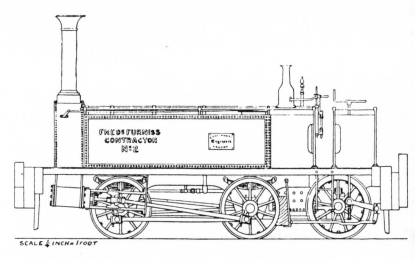

SCALE ¼ INCH = 1 FOOT

George England's early version of a contractor's engine

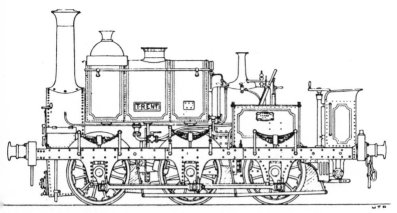

The former Great Northern Railway 2-2-2 after rebuilding as a 0-6-0ST in 1871. *Trent* worked at Dartford on a James Rennie contract and on the Central Wales Railway

Boulton in the following year, who resold her to the North Staffordshire Iron Company.

Specially built contractor's engines, as distinct from rebuilds, were a speciality of George England & Co of Hatcham Ironworks, Camberwell. These were small, cabless 0-4-0 side tank engines with outside cylinders. The contractor of the Hayling Island branch, Frederick Furniss of Havant, had one of these engines, to which was added a pair of trailing wheels so that it could run the passenger service on that beloved railway, presumably so that it did not become uncoupled, as 0-4-0 tank engines were wont to do.

The contractors who emerged and expanded from the holocaust of 1866 were much more diversified than their predecessors, but they still had to rely on steam-hauled railways for carting spoil inland away from docks and other contracts, as well as from the railway contracts that they undertook. Messrs Logan & Hemingway built many lines for the Manchester, Sheffield & Lincolnshire Railway from the early 1870s until the London Extension was completed. For this and other jobs they employed a large fleet of 0-4-0 and 0-6-0 saddle tanks, built almost exclusively by Manning Wardle. One of the 0-6-0s, *Sir Berkeley*, formerly No 11 in the Logan & Hemingway fleet, survives on the Keighley & Worth Valley Railway. Manning Wardle became the standard suppliers of contractors' engines for about half a century, so appropriate was their basic tank engine design. Much of Logan & Hemingway's work at the turn of the century was for the MSLR, especially the London Extension and docks on Humberside with connecting railways. Sheds to house and maintain the engines used were built at Staveley and Grimsby for the respective projects. As contracts were completed, engines were transferred to new sites, so that at any one time there might be thirty or more locomotives at work on a number of contracts.

Contractors' locomotives, affectionately known as 'Pugs', had to stand up to some rough treatment. The trackbed was very uneven, both vertically and laterally, so jacks were essential for quick rerailing of engines and trucks. Tipping wagons were often braked by means of 'spragging', using a tapering block of wood which was thrust between the wheels to bring the trucks to an abrupt halt – with one more flat on their tyres. The driver of the Pug had to act simultaneously if he was to avoid an accident as the train skidded to a snatched halt, often on greasy rails. The movements of a well-coordinated team became almost balletic, but errors led to derailments, delays, injury and even death.

The engines themselves suffered dislocated boiler tubes and springs. The latter merely made the ride even rougher till a visit to the blacksmith could be postponed no longer, but leaking tubes meant less power, so first-aid in the form of a generous dose of bran was staple treatment, blocking the holes until a more permanent remedy could be obtained. Duncan Kennedy, an engineering assistant to the contractor on the Ballachulish line, remembered one occasion when there was no bran, so the driver followed a horse until it performed and then emptied the droppings into the boiler, to good effect.

Another contractor with a large semi-permanent fleet was Sir Thomas Firbank, many of whose locomotives were photographed by Newton of Leicester while at work on the Marylebone contracts. He also had a small fleet of narrow gauge engines at work in the Delabole slate quarries in north Cornwall.

Eventually, though, the development of rubber-tyred scrapers, dump trucks and caterpillar tracks made the use of locomotives even for railway work redundant.

Epilogue – Railway Contracting in Recent Years

Few new railways or even major bridges and tunnels have been built in the last seventy years, yet there has been a continuous demand for contractors' services to remodel goods yards, rebuild stations, replace level crossings with bridges, widen lines, strengthen bridges, reline tunnels and a hundred and one other jobs too large for the railways' own maintenance staff. The specialised railway contractor has either diversified or disappeared, but his successor, the civil engineering conglomerates and groups of today, can tackle the major works as they become available, usually as part of government-aid packages for modernisation, beginning in the mid-1950s.

Civil engineering companies such as McAlpines, Taylor Woodrow and Monks differ markedly from the nineteenth-century railway builders. The former are usually public companies with a large capital. Their headquarters and depots are permanent, with large salaried staffs and research units working at the frontiers of constructional expertise. Their activities are spread across the whole span of civil engineering, so that a company like Taylor Woodrow was engaged in the Euston Station redevelopment between 1962 and 1968 while simultaneously constructing motorways, tower blocks, nuclear power stations, docks, factory estates and mines in all continents except Antarctica.

Such companies are enormously strong, so that the failure of even a major contract will not bring down the company as a whole. Although most were founded by masterful individuals, few rely any longer on a single outstanding character for their continued success. The problems with costing and completion that still plague the industry are inevitable results of inflation of material and labour costs, but also because the long lead times make the number of unknowable variables so much greater.

The size of modern civil engineering contractors can be judged by the strength of their work-force and the valuation of their capital by the Stock Exchange. One of the largest is the Tarmac group, which includes the pioneering railway contractors Messrs Cubitts. This company has 26,688 employees and a capital value of £250m. Taylor Woodrow has over 10,000 employees and a value of £150m, dwarfing A. Monk & Co of Warrington, which is diverting the East Coast main line around the Selby coalfield. This rare example of several miles of main-line construction is on a scale similar to a motorway contract in its earthmoving and bridge-building requirements. The company employs about 4,000 people and is valued at £7m. All these are capable of expansion and contraction, and few would be found on a railway contract at any one time, given the level of business as well as the sheer diversity of civil engineering contracts in which any one firm might be engaged. Some idea of the size of single contracts can be gained from the recent award to Taylor Woodrow of the £40m contract for the Phase II of the Trans Gabon Railway in Central Africa.

Balfour Beatty, part of the BICC electrical group, specialises in rail electrification. Its team of eighty erectors worked on the Moorgate to Bedford system until 1982. Should the plans proposed for nationwide electrification be commenced, their future will be bright indeed. Already plans to electrify the lines from Colchester to Norwich and Harwich have been confirmed, while the East Coast main-line contract seems likely, a job so large that much larger contracts may well have to be placed with other contractors already mentioned.

All this is a very long way from the men of a century and a half ago who pioneered the large-scale project with a rough and ready labour force, operating manually with money placed at their disposal by a country banker. Railways made the emergence of the civil engineering contractor possible on a large scale.

APPENDIX I

Statement of Sir Morton Peto's Affairs, *The Economist*, 1866

. . . he borrowed at rates of interest so high as to be injurious to his credit as well as destructive of his profit. Still the immense mass of his business was very good, and some of it doubtless stupendously profitable. There was no lending of millions on securities not worth thousands. That the last few weeks must have been very painful to Sir Morton Peto we can well believe, but no one can doubt who really understands such matters that he will emerge from the cloud still a very rich man, and with a character for honour beyond the reach of any question.

The statement of the affairs of Messrs Peto, Betts, and Co. is as follows:

STATEMENT of the AFFAIRS of Messrs PETO and BETTS, May 10, 1866.

	£ s d	£ s d	£ s d
To creditors unsecured			258,948 18 6
To creditors holding security (partly covered), amount of claims		15,000 0 0	
Estimated value of security held		14,997 10 0	
			2 10 0
To creditors holding security (fully covered), amount of claims		375,900 3 0	
Estimated value of security		509,104 0 0	
Surplus contra		132,203 17 0	
Further creditors, fully covered claims		119,000 0 0	
Estimated value of security		136,576 0 0	
Surplus deducted from liabilities below		17,576 0 0	
To liabilities on account of James M'Henry, not covered by any security from him		227,000 0 0	
Less: – Securities deposited by Peto and Betts	30,000 0 0		
Surplus from creditors holding security, who also hold some of these liabilities	17,576 0 0	47,576 0 0	
			179,424 0 0

To liabilities on account of James M'Henry, covered by Atlantic and Great Western bonds and debentures	104,000	0	0			
To liabilities on bills to be provided for by other parties	83,000	0	0			
To liabilities on bills receivable	68,450	1	8			
				438,375	8	6
By cash at bankers				7,744	15	11
By debtors				7,750	7	2
By securities in hand				66,781	0	0
By plant				52,800	0	0
By surplus from creditors holding security, per contra				132,203	17	0
Deferred assets, viz.:						
Advances on works, after allowing for contingencies				574,349	1	0
Debt due from James M'Henry, after charging him with 227,000*l* per contra				293,867	4	7
Balance of advances in respect of works which are being carried out by other parties				185,300	0	0
Sundry assets				153,268	8	2
Interest on freehold and leasehold properties				88,000	0	0
Total				1,562,064	13	10

APPENDIX II

Railway Building Statistics and Profitability in Years of Major Railway Contracts, *The Economist*, 1866

Year	Capital Expended on Railways open for Traffic £	Average Cost per mile £	Total Traffic Receipts £	Average Receipts per mile for the Year £
1842	54,380,100	33,162	4,470,700	2,743
1843	60,637,100	34,929	5,022,650	2,805
1844	66,882,100	34,290	5,814,980	2,982
1845	75,646,100	33,736	6,909,270	3,080
1846	87,765,100	30,903	7,945,870	2,797
1847	114,728,000	30,924	9,277,670	2,501
1848	154,200,000	33,333	10,445,100	2,258
1849	197,000,000	33,110	11,683,800	2,000
1850	230,522,730	34,236	13,142,235	1,944
1851	236,841,420	34,186	14,987,310	2,163
1852	248,033,520	33,816	15,543,610	2,118
1853	263,636,320	33,912	17,920,530	2,305
1854	273,860,000	34,113	20,000,000	2,491
1855	291,903,000	35,425	21,123,315	2,567
1856	298,946,260	34,122	22,995,500	2,625
1857	307,153,670	33,492	24,162,465	2,634
1858	315,950,000	33,000	23,763,764	2,484
1859	322,219,100	32,603	25,576,100	2,588
1860	329,827,200	32,106	27,576,783	2,685
1861	342,386,100	31,633	28,268,374	2,614
1862	355,167,280	31,118	28,850,612	2,532
1863	373,246,200	31,354	30,498,660	2,532
1864	391,396,680	31,209	33,182,497	2,646
1865	412,558,100	31,801	35,335,838	2,724
1866	446,746,800	33,272	37,415,927	2,713

Year	Working Expenses, Rates and Taxes Per cent	Length of Line open at end of Year Miles	Per Centage of Traffic Receipts on Capital Expended Per cent	Per Centage of Profit on Capital Expended Per cent
1842	40	1,630	8.22	4.93
1843	40	1,730	8.28	4.94
1844	40	1,950	8.70	5.22
1845	40	2,243	9.13	5.48
1846	42	2,840	9.05	5.25
1847	42	3,710	8.08	4.69
1848	42	4,626	6.77	4.06
1849	42	5,950	5.93	3.44
1850	42	6,733	5.70	3.31
1851	42	6,928	6.32	3.67
1852	45	7.337	6.27	3.41
1853	44	7,774	6.80	3.80
1854	46	8,028	7.30	3.53
1855	47	8,240	7.24	3.90
1856	48	8,761	7.69	4.00
1857	48	9,171	7.87	4.19
1858	48	9,568	7.52	3.91
1859	48	9,883	7.94	4.13
1860	47.5	10,273	8.37	4.39
1861	48	10,811	8.27	4.30
1862	48	11,386	8.12	4.22
1863	48	11,904	8.17	4.25
1864	47	12,582	8.48	4.49
1865	48	12,973	8.57	4.46
1866	48.8	13,424	8.38	4.29

APPENDIX III

Advertisements to Contractors, *Stamford Mercury*, 1846

LONDON & NORTH WESTERN RAILWAY,
RUGBY AND STAMFORD BRANCH

The Directors of the London & North Western Railway Company will meet at the Company's Offices, Euston Station, London, on Wednesday the 18th day of November next, at One o'clock in the Afternoon to receive Tenders for the construction of the following Divisions of the said Rugby & Stamford Branch Railway; videlicet –

Contract No 1 – Commencing at the Rugby station of the London & North Western Railway, and terminating in a Field in the parish of Theddingworth in the county of Leicester, numbered 34 in the Plan of the said Rugby & Stamford Railway deposited with the Clerk of the Peace in the same county, being a distance of thirteen miles or thereabouts.

Contract No 4 – Commencing in a Field in the parish of Lyddington in the county of Rutland, numbered 8 in the said Plan deposited with the Clerk of the Peace for the same county and terminating at the junction of the Peterborough & Syston Railway in the parish of South Luffenham, in the county of Rutland, at the point marked R on the said Plan deposited with the Clerk of the Peace for the same county.

The contracts will comprise the execution of all the Excavations, Embankments, Bridges, Tunnels, and other works, and laying the permanent way and maintenance of works for twelve calendar months after completion.

Plans, Sections, Drawings, and Specifications, and general conditions, together with Draft of a Contract which will be required to be entered into, will be ready at the Engineer's Office, No 3, Princes St, Westminster, for the inspection of parties proposing to tender, on Wednesday, the 4th day of November, where they are requested to meet the Engineer at 10 o'clock a.m. on that day.

No Tender will be received at Euston Station after One o'clock on the 18th day of November.

The parties tendering, or their authorised Agents, must be in attendance.

The Directors do not bind themselves to accept the lowest Tender.

By order,
R. Creed, Secretary.

The Pearson Contract for GWR, South Wales Direct Railway – Detailed Estimate for Tunnel

TUNNEL No. 3

		at	£	s	d
319,836 cubic yds.	Excavation for tunnel measured to back of brickwork, including all timbering, pumping and other contingencies as specified	8/-	127,934	8	0
26,136	Brickwork in mortar in side walls, including all cleaning and pointing				
37,752 · 70,488 cubic yds.	Ditto in arch, including centering and all cleaning and pointing	31/-	109,256	8	0
6,600	Brickwork in mortar in invert, including all cleaning and pointing				
10,220 cubic yds.	Excavation for ditto	8/-	4,088	0	0
133 lin. ft.	Blue brick label course, 1ft. 6in. by 6in. by 6in.	2/3	14	19	3
103 lin. ft.	Extra only to string course	1/-	5	3	0
288 cubic ft.	Pennant stone coping	4/-	57	12	0
478 cubic yds.	Masonry in mortar in face-work of tunnel, including all cleaning and pointing	24/-	573	12	0
278 cubic yds.	Excavation in foundations and slopes for facework of tunnel	3/-	41	14	0
48 lin. ft.	3in. earthenware pipes in weep holes	6d	1	4	0
50 cubic yds.	Lime concrete in foundations	15/-	37	10	0
			£242,010	10	3

Notes

Introduction
1   A. Trollope, *Doctor Thorne*

Chapter 2
1   J. Francis, *History of the English Railway* (1851), p229
2   Anon *Stokers and Pokers* (1846), p23
3   *Ibid*, p23
4   *Ibid*, p23
5   A Civil Engineer *Personal Recollections of English Engineers* (1868), p18
6   *Ibid*, p181
7   J. Francis, op cit

Chapter 3
1   J. Francis, op cit, p50
2   J. Devey, *The Life of Joseph Locke* (1862)
3   Sir J. Rennie, *Autobiography*
4   *Ibid*
5   Select Committee Report (1846)
6   Select Committee Report (1846)
7   J. A. Patmore, *Journal of Transport History* (1962)

Chapter 4
1   Select Committee Report (1846)
2   A. Helps, *Life & Labours of Mr Brassey*
3   Parliamentary Select Committee 1846
4   *Ibid*
5   Bradshaw's Manual 1855
6   J. Devey, *The Life of Joseph Locke* (1862)
7   *Illustrated London News* (1859)
8   *Ibid*
9   LTSR Annual Report 1912
10   A. Helps, op cit
11   J. Devey, op cit
12   A. Helps, op cit

Chapter 6
1   A. Helps, op cit

Chapter 8
1   F. Fox, *Sixty-three years of Engineering* (1921)
2   T. Walker, *The Severn Tunnel; Its construction & difficulties* (1891)
3   *Ibid*
4   *Ibid*
5   *Ibid*
6   *Ibid*
7   *Ibid*
8   *Ibid*
9   *Ibid*
10 *Ibid*
11 Sir J. Hawkshaw, Proceedings Institute of Civil Engineers, Obituaries, 1891

Chapter 9
1   Economist Law Report, 1866
2   The Essex Standard, 1866

Bibliography

Primary Sources
Minute Books, Engineers' Reports and Annual Reports of the pre-grouping railway companies (Public Record Office)
Board of Trade Reports made prior to railways opening (Public Record Office)
Railway Returns
Select Committee on Railway Labourers, Parliamentary Papers 1846 XIII

Journals and Magazines
Builder
Diss Express
The Economist
Engineer
Engineering
Herapath's
Illustrated London News
Journal of Transport History
Minutes of the Proceedings of the Institute of Civil Engineers
Norfolk Chronicle
Railway Magazine
Railway Times
Transport History

Secondary Sources
Barman, C. *Introduction to Railway Architecture* (London Art and Technics, 1950)
Baughan, P. *North of Leeds* (Roundhouse, 1966)
Baxter, B. *Stone Blocks and Iron Rails* (David & Charles, 1966)
Coleman, T. *The Railway Navvies* (Hutchinson, 1965)
Devey, J. *The Life of Joseph Locke* (1862)
Dow, G. *Great Central*, Vols 1, 2 and 3 (Ian Allan, 1959, 1962, 1971)
Fairbairn, W. *An Account of the Construction of the Britannia and Conway Tubular Bridges* (1849)
Fox, F. *Sixty-three Years of Engineering* (1921)
Francis, J. *A History of the English Railway* (1851)
Hadfield, C. *The Canals of South Wales and the Border* (David & Charles, 1960)

Helps, A. *The Life and Labours of Mr Brassey* (1872)

Jenks, L. H. *Migration of British Capital* (1927)

Kellett, J. R. *Impact of Railways on Victorian Cities* (Routledge & Kegan Paul, 1969)

Kennedy, Duncan. *The Birth and Death of a Highland Railway* (John Murray, 1971)

Lecount, P. *History of the Railway Connecting London & Birmingham* (1839)

Lewin, H. *The Railway Mania and its Aftermath* (1936)

McDermott, F. *The Life and Work of Joseph Firbank* (1887)

Mackay, T. *The Life of Sir John Fowler* (1900)

Marshall, J. *A Biographical Dictionary of Railway Engineers* (David & Charles, 1978)

Moore, R. *Paddy Waddell's Railway* (1973)

Peto, H. *Sir Morton Peto* (1893)

Pole, W. *The Life of William Fairbairn* (1877)

Pollins, H. *Britain's Railways: An Industrial History* (David & Charles, 1971)

Reed, M. C. (ed) *Railways in the Victorian Economy* (David & Charles, 1969)

Rolt, L. *Isambard Kingdom Brunel* (Longman, 1962)

Rolt, L. *George & Robert Stephenson* (Longman, 1960)

Skeat, W. *George Stephenson* (Institute of Mechanical Engineers, 1973)

Spender, J. *Weetman Pearson* (1930)

Tatlow, J. *Fifty Years of Railway Life* (1920)

Thomas, I. *Top Sawyer* (1938)

Thomas, J. *The Tay Bridge Disaster* (David & Charles, 1972)

Vignoles, O. *The Life of Charles Blacker Vignoles* (1889)

Walker, T. *The Severn Tunnel* (1891)

Williams, F. *The Midland Railway* (1876)

Acknowledgements

My grateful thanks go to the many libraries and their staff who have helped me to locate the books, journals and records that have provided me with the raw material for this book: the Public Record Office, Kew; the reference libraries and record offices of Norfolk, the City of Westminster and Leicester, the National Railway Museum, York; the Museum of Wales; the universities of Leicester, East Anglia and London; and Lens of Sutton. All have contributed greatly to both word and picture; comfort, warmth, quiet and unobtrusive helpfulness characterise these institutions, which make work a pleasure.

Helpful advice from Professor Alan Patmore of Hull, Dr David Brooke of Bath, Hugh Fenwick of BR, York, and David St John Thomas have materially aided the author, but responsibility for the contents is entirely my own.

Index